SETTING
THE
CAPTIVES
FREE

SETTING THE CAPTIVES FREE

*Victims of the Church
Tell Their Stories*

BY AUSTIN MILES
Author of "Don't Call Me Brother"

PROMETHEUS BOOKS
Buffalo, New York

Library of Congress Cataloging-in-Publication Data

Miles, Austin, 1933-
    Setting the captives free : victims of the church tell their stories / Austin Miles.
        p.   cm.
    Includes index.
    ISBN 0-87975-617
    1. Miles, Austin, 1933-   . 2. Miles, Austin, 1933-   —
Correspondence. 3. Assemblies of God—Controversial literature.
4. Pentecostal churches—Controversial literature. 5. Pentecostals—United
States—Correspondence. 6. Ex-church members—United States—
Correspondence. 7. Miles, Austin, 1933-   Don't call me brother.
I. Title.
BX8765.5.Z5M56   1990
289.9′4′092—dc20
[B]   90-41249
                                                          CIP

This book is dedicated to the FBI, whose constant surveillance of my life helped keep me on the straight and narrow. You helped make me what I am today.

Therefore my people are gone into captivity, because they have no knowledge.

Isaiah 5:13

Contents

Acknowledgments

The author is grateful to Irene and Don McGee, whose friendship and financial assistance during the restructuring of my life will never be forgotten; to William Kastell, who continually scouted the flea markets and kept me supplied with portable typewriters; and to Nancy Schiller, my watchful editor at Prometheus.

Preface

Guilty on all twenty-four counts of mail fraud, wire fraud, and conspiracy. On October 5, 1989, Jim Bakker became the first major television evangelist to be convicted of a felony in connection with his ministry. Along with this landmark decision, the taboo of questioning or criticizing religious enterprises and their leaders finally came tumbling down like the walls of Jericho. The trumpet had clearly sounded from both an incensed public that had become sick of the deceptions of Corporate Christianity, and from the federal government, which had long avoided any kind of involvement in the sensitive area of religion, crooked or not.

Until recently, efforts to expose any ministry were met with hostility from the public at large. I experienced extreme pressure while attempting to expose Jim Bakker's homosexuality and fundraising scams a year before the Jessica Hahn scandal broke. Nobody wanted to hear it, much less believe it.

Many attempts were made to sabotage and stop the publication of my book *Don't Call Me Brother*. The greatest intimidation came from a television preacher who was barely mentioned in that book. After gaining access to advance galleys, his lawyers threatened to bankrupt Prometheus if the book were published. The publisher received harassing telephone calls almost daily. During that same time, I received a death threat.

Likewise, anyone who would publicize the book was hounded by this man's lawyers. Pressure was put on "Entertainment Tonight" not to air a piece about the book that it had taped on February 21, 1989. Its "Inside Story" finally did air six weeks later, on April 6, 1989.

The office of a major newspaper that had prepared a story about the conflict was visited by the entire board of directors of that ministry. As a result of the visit, the newspaper killed the story. Other newspapers were similarly persuaded to write nothing about the author or the book.

The struggle to tell my story in *Don't Call Me Brother* would not have been complete without some dirty tricks perpetrated by individuals who were *not* among the righteous. The *Charlotte Observer* obtained advance galleys from the publisher under the pretext of wanting to do a review of the book. From there copies were made (without permission) by *Observer* reporters and distributed to people who were named in the book. This resulted in several threats of lawsuits. Prometheus could very well have knuckled under and canceled the project. Fortunately for everyone it did not. At one point, the presses were shut down while a libel lawyer carefully examined the manuscript, which delayed the original publication date of April 19, 1989. The book's documentation was declared valid, the manuscript (with only a couple of minor alterations) was given a clean bill of health, and the presses were turned back on.

In the meantime, the newspaper was preparing to publish its own version of the Bakker scandals in a book by one of its star reporters. Any doubt about their motives was put to rest on April 6, 1989, when the *Charlotte Observer* published a "review" of *Don't Call Me Brother* that claimed the book was not documented, corroborated, or even truthful. In a classic example of overkill, the "review" went so far as to refer to me as "sleaze." Exactly two weeks later, on August 20, 1989, the same newspaper put out a release on the Associated Press wire about its own book, expected to be published a month later, which they described as "thoroughly documented," the efforts of two years of research by their own Pulitzer Prize-winning reporter.

Reactions to *Don't Call Me Brother* have been strong. There seems to be no neutral ground. Many of the people who have read the book have felt compelled to respond. And, as was expected, there have been many public statements on it. The Assemblies of God published a paper which they sent to their ministers instructing them to have nothing to do with *Don't Call Me Brother*, as ". . . it is filled with inaccuracies and prejudicial statements." The letter was dated April 10, 1989. The book itself was not even published until May 15, 1989.

Before his conviction, Jim Bakker told his TV-ministry audience not to spend their money "to buy that book," but to give it to him instead for his ministry. In an interview on "The Jack Cole Show" on WJNO Radio in West Palm Beach, Florida, "Dr." Robert Schuller (as he likes to be called) referred to the work as ". . . that tragic book just filled with lies." Schuller became so rattled during that surprise-twist interview that "the positive thinker" tried to walk out six times. Careful preparations had been made for Schuller's hastily arranged visit to WJNO. With superb investigative skill, Jill Mather-Bowen, a producer of WJNO, racing against time, gathered an amazing file on Schuller's misleading fundraising schemes and his opulent lifestyle. In the hands of the free-spirited, irreverent Jack Cole the information resulted in one of radio's finest hours. That November 6, 1989, broadcast has been preserved for posterity, has been rebroadcast, and will be again. Schuller is still furious with all of us. If truth hurts, then the man in the glass house is in agony.

Followers of the late esteemed faith healer Rev. William Branham sent out mass mailings in an attempt to organize an international protest against Prometheus and myself. Donna Rice threatened to sue over the reference to her relationship with born-again stunt man Bobby Yerkes. In her letter to Prometheus she said it could damage her reputation. Yerkes grumbled to Hollywood theatrical agent Gil Miller: "I'm not going to call him and yell at him, it won't do any good."

Through it all, not one lawsuit was ever actually filed.

Once *Don't Call Me Brother* hit the bookstores, the response was immediate, and it still continues daily. The reaction, tone, and content of the letters I have received have surprised everyone connected with the project. Regardless of which side of the religious fence the reader is on, these letters will prove fascinating. Each one is a mini-book of its own, as the writers pour out their thoughts, experiences, anguish, and passion concerning one of the deepest emotions ever implanted in the human mind—the need to believe in religion, in God, and in those who claim to be God's "anointed."

It is by public demand that this sequel is being published, along with the letters of response. *Don't Call Me Brother* created quite a stir in all circles and, along with the controversy, aroused in everyone a curiosity that demanded to be satisfied. "What did people in general *really* think about the book?" was asked over and over. This book will answer that question—and others.

To many readers, these revealing letters will be a healing, as they affirm the questions and suspicions that have long puzzled all of us. Some of the letters will cause readers to shake their heads in disbelief. Other letters take the author to task with pointed, accusing questions. I have reproduced the letters exactly as they were written, except for some corrections in spelling. Several names and places have been disguised to protect the writers.

All in all, the powerful letters contained in these pages, written by people from different parts of the world, people with varied backgrounds and lifestyles, all point to an overwhelming truth about the church, a truth that just might help in *Setting the Captives Free*. If that can be accomplished, then the destructive church experience I and many others suffered will not have been in vain.

Austin Miles

San Francisco, California
April 1990

I

A Man of Letters

Oh that my words were now written! Oh that they were printed in a book!

Job 19:23

During 1988, a prominent church near Concord, California, announced these glad tidings of great joy in its church bulletin: "Bring your pets this Sunday at 2:00 for the annual Blessing Of The Animals. This will be followed by a barbeque." Behold, a truth! Go to church for a blessing and get slaughtered. This theme is all too prevalent in the letters you are about to read. The first one is an open, very personal letter from the wife of a former Assemblies of God minister who now lives in Colorado.

Sunday, August 13, 1989
5:00 P.M.

Dear Mr. Miles:

I started reading your book *Don't Call Me Brother* at 7:45 this morning and finished it about a half hour ago. Although I had work to do today at my bookkeeping business, and laundry besides, there is no way I could put your book down. You told the story of my life experience with the Assemblies of God.

I don't want to bore you with more horror stories, but I want to share this with you and to say thank you. Until now, I've had the recurring thought in the back of my head that maybe they were right—maybe there's something wrong with me.

I was raised A.G. My mom was converted shortly after she married my dad, whose father was an A.G. pastor for years—he saved souls on Sunday and verbally and physically abused his wife and 7 children the rest of the week, all who are dysfunctional to this day.

My mom's salvation put a big gulf between her and my dad. They're still married, but both are extremely unhappy. My dad thinks he's been cheated because mom is no fun—mom has been cheated out of having a happy Christian home. They've raised 6 children in this atmosphere, who are also dysfunctional.

I grew up a rebel, mostly inside, but I did my share of beer parties and sex with boys I didn't even know. I lost my virginity before I was 9 to an uncle 6 years older than me. I enjoyed the attention (my dad basically ignored me) until it became a pretty big burden. So I told my parents— my mom blamed me.

I spent the next years of my life trying to redeem myself with my mom, without succeeding, until I got saved. As far as she's concerned, you aren't acceptable if you aren't saved. My dad was good to us, but Mom let us know that no matter how good he was, he was unacceptable because he wasn't saved.

I went to church quite a bit during jr. high and high school, and was fed full of the "don'ts"—don't date, don't wear make-up, don't dance, don't go to movies, don't wear jeans or shorts, don't play cards, don't cut your hair, don't drink, don't smoke, don't kiss —and you'll end up in hell for sure if you have sex before you're married.

According to them I was already doomed—so I tried all the harder. Every time there was an altar call, I went down— and repented—and repented—and repented.

Somewhere about 16 I decided there was no point and quit going to church. I lived with my mother's disapproval until May 1, 1970—8 days before my 21st birthday.

On that evening the new pastor of the A.G. church in town and his wife came to see me. I had been dating a black baseball player, and was falling in love with him. Our small town was extremely prejudiced and I wondered what God had to say about it. I never found out—the pastor got onto salvation and wouldn't leave until I got on my knees and named every sin I could think of and repented of it. It was after midnight. I didn't feel wonderful, or great, or relieved, or holy, only tired.

I tried very hard in the next 3 years to play the game. I did what they told me, dressed like they told me, talked like they told me. I went to church every time the doors opened, I tithed and gave, I clapped and sang and cried and prayed, but I didn't know God—or Jesus Christ. So—I clapped and prayed all the harder, still repenting every chance I got.

I met my future husband around Thanksgiving 1972, where else but church? I fell hard, but never felt worthy of him. He had not done all the horrible things I had done; he was gentle and everyone liked him. And—most of all— he had a CALL on his life, God had called him into THE MINISTRY!!! This did not particularly bother me until I realized that in order for this to happen, I would have to go through a total transformation—I was totally unacceptable as a pastor's wife.

So the "transformation" began. I attended weekly counseling sessions with the pastor, went to pastors' retreats and meetings with Matthew (my fiance) and attended more religious services than I could count. I could only associate with Christians, so I dropped my other friends, one by one. The church became my whole life—but I was dead inside. I had no assurance that God even knew who I was; if He did, I was sure He didn't like me—I was unacceptable.

The biggest problem I had with A.G. leadership was my unwillingness to accept whatever they put out just because they said so. I asked questions, and I expected answers, real ones, not just A.G. doctrine or rules. My goal was to know God, not climb the A.G. ladder to success.

Matthew and I got married anyway, even if I wasn't exactly a model pastor's wife, and moved to Minneapolis so Matthew could go to Bible school.

Until that time, Matthew was inclined to go along with the A.G. pastor's wife definition—you know what I'm talking about, you've seen plenty of them. He couldn't understand why I was so set on rocking the boat. He had a pretty low self-esteem and he had visions of grandeur fueled by the A.G. leadership's assurance of a "high" call of God on his life.

To be frank, life in Minneapolis was hell! Here I was, a newlywed, away from home for the first time, with a husband who could only think of the church, the church. I had a very clear distinction between God and the church— Matthew and almost every preacher (and preacher's wife) I've met saw them as the same thing. That gave them license to neglect their families in order to build churches "for God." And do you know, most of their wives accepted, no, they *encouraged* this behavior, and became martyrs themselves, "for God."

When Matthew started doing this as a youth pastor in a small Iowa church, I came unglued. At the time we had our 2 children, a girl, 1, and a newborn son, and I needed help. But Matthew was off saving souls and counseling. To make it worse, everyone assured me he was doing the right thing and I had better get used to it. One pastor, hearing me complain, went so far as to tell Matthew he'd better get me under control or I'd ruin his ministry.

Those were the loneliest and most unhappy years of my life. I went through the motions as best I could, but inside I felt hurt, mad, and most of all betrayed by a God and a man, who both were supposed to love me. It finally got to the point where I sat down in my chair and vowed not to get up until I knew God was real. I sat there 2 days and got no answers, so I got up—I had kids to take care of. But something died inside—if there was a God, He didn't care about me. I was just handy; Matthew needed a wife and I was available—the sacrifice for his ministry—his church.

Then a couple came into our lives, sent to us directly by God, who loved us—both of us, not just Matthew. They recognized my value as a person in my own right. For the first time I saw the love of God shine through a person in the form of total acceptance and total approval—just as I was. They were *not* A.G.

We left the Assemblies of God and submitted ourselves

to the ministry of this couple for the next 4 years. A lot of healing took place in me and Matthew learned a lot, about priorities and about the difference between God and the church. I credit that couple with saving our marriage.

At the end of 3 years we went back to the Assemblies of God, and sat in a very large church for 2 years, before the pastor admitted to adultery and left the church October 1983. It was hard for the church, but somehow we were personally spared. We loved him and still do, but we weren't looking to any man for that heavy degree of leadership we had before.

Two years later we submitted to the interrogation that A.G. puts its ministers through. I felt that it was degrading, but did it for Matthew. After all, he had this "call," and I was still intimidated by it.

Because our former pastor was Asst. District Superintendent, and I wasn't on very good terms with him (I was not "submissive"), we applied for and got a small church in the Colorado mountains.

In this beautiful setting I was forced to personally start cutting through the garbage and come face to face with God.

I had come to Colorado as—once again—a martyr *and* as a submissive wife. Back in Des Moines I had been going to college—to get a degree in accounting and become a CPA, a lifelong dream. We moved Aug. 85, just after I had been awarded an $8,000/year scholarship to Drake University. Knowing how badly Matthew wanted to pastor, and assured that God would reward my sacrifice, I turned it down.

I was rewarded all right. I moved from a fair-sized city, with all its shopping conveniences, to a town of 1800 (during hunting season), over a mountain and 120 miles from anywhere. Everyone wore cowboy boots and carried a gun in their pickup. There were no sidewalks and all we could find to live in was a trailer with a roof that vibrated in the wind. Everyone was either a rancher, a logger or worked for the railroad. College was out, and neither of us could find work. The 40 families who were supposed to be supporting us turned out to be 4, and the pastor in the next town, who had brought us there did just that—brought us there and left us on our own.

I came unglued—I was furious—with Matthew, with the town, with the pastor in the next town, with the Assemblies of God, and with God Himself. I screamed and bawled and broke things and threatened lives—here I was being sacrificed again for a stupid church.

I have to relate one incident to you—it was the only satisfaction I had for over a year. The pastor from the next town (the one who brought us out there) and his wife stopped by one day. I was not in a particularly good mood, but I felt obligated to invite them in and at least be cordial. The four of us made small talk for a while, then they asked me how I was doing. I told them—directly and to the point. In there somewhere I mentioned that I was mad at God. The pastor's wife, good little Christian that she was, assured me this was not possible—no one who loved God could be mad at Him; it just wasn't done. I assured her that that was indeed the situation, and she just wouldn't let it drop. I had several months of anger, rejection and betrayal stored up, so I let her have it—verbally. At that point her husband felt obligated to step in, since Matthew hadn't made any attempt to get his wife under control. He got up and started toward me, saying something about praying for me (when all else fails, pastors resort to prayer). I told him to stay away from me, not to touch me, and he'd better not dare pray for me. By this time his wife was on her way to the car—she probably thought I was demon-possessed.

I felt wonderful. Right or wrong, I had been honest and had stood up for myself—and to a preacher. They never came to our house again.

Matthew did eventually get a job in November and I got one 1½ years later, and we pastored our church.

One thing we picked up right away. No one in the district headquarters in Denver cared about us and our 25 people—unless we played the game. First of all, in spite of severe financial circumstances, we were expected to attend all pastor's conferences, fellowships, and district meetings. Matthew did, once in a while when his work schedule permitted, but I wouldn't go at all. Those people are about as real as stone statues in a museum. Then we were expected to have evangelists and missionaries in to speak. Our church couldn't even pay rent on a building—there was no way it could pay a special speaker; no one came for free. And—most of all—they wanted us to put up a building. The only regular tithers we had were ourselves, and we couldn't afford to make payments on a building.

When the district saw that we wouldn't play, they left us alone—totally. We received no support, no fellowship, no encouragement. But—we were offered a bigger church after 2 years. I guess we had proved ourselves somehow by sticking it out that long in a little cow town, so they gave us the opportunity to start our own climb to the top. We said "no thank you" and stayed another year. In that time our people started going to another "full gospel" church in town, and we felt released to move on. In that time we had also bought a bookkeeping business about 40 miles away, so we moved there. The pastor who hired us took a bigger church, with a Christian school, the next step on his ladder.

And we got off. When it came time to renew Matthew's license, they wrote and told us that we "owed" the district some money in unpaid tithes and they wouldn't renew his license until we paid. We decided that if we had to pay to do God's will, there was something definitely wrong—so we once again said "no, thank you."

We haven't been to church since January 88, and haven't missed it. We were pursued for awhile, but I'm sure we've been written off my now, and I'm glad.

What's encouraging to me is that I have a better relationship with God, the PERSON, than ever. How it began was I heard someone talking about standing naked before God. My first reaction to that was, "Puke! No way!" But the thought wouldn't leave. As I mulled it over, it occurred to me that God saw me that way anyway, and more. He knew my thoughts and He knew what was in my heart. So I decided to try it. As I was alone one day I sat in my favorite chair and came to God—naked. I told Him I wasn't sure about the Bible. I knew He wrote it, but I also knew stupid ego-centered men had interpreted it and I felt they had screwed up its meaning horribly and had used it to manipulate people and build empires for themselves.

I told Him I didn't mind talking to Him, but that I had

no idea how to pray. Most of what I had learned about praying was used to try to manipulate Him—as if anyone could.

So I wasn't going to read or pray anymore, but I would do my best to come before Him naked and be honest. In return I expected Him to be honest with me.

Then I did something else. I told Him I knew there were places in my life that needed to be healed—places I didn't want to look at and some that I was unable to look at. But I wanted Him to look at them. I wanted Him to see all of me—inside and out—to see if He could still love and accept and even approve of me if He saw it all.

He did! Not right then, and I didn't get any tingles or see lights, nor was I slain in the Spirit. I didn't see or hear anything. In fact, I sort of forgot I'd even said it. But every once in a while, I'd think of something I'd done that made me feel unacceptable, and it didn't hurt. I felt no shame. I didn't feel the need to repent again. I wasn't happy about it, but I didn't feel degraded or second-class.

That's where I am. My mom and some of my brothers and sisters still go to the A.G. church in their town, but I won't go. That man is evil, building himself an empire in God's name. He's destined to fall, and hard. I tell my family that every chance I get. So far, they haven't listened. Like 90% of the "Christians," they equate God with the church and feel they must go to be saved. Anyway why wouldn't they? They're told that from the time they get there until they leave. They also look at a pastor as only slightly lower than God and a lot more accessible. This boosts the pastor's ego, so he's careful to maintain and encourage that concept.

I love God so much, and it breaks my heart to see what's happening. There's going to be a lot of surprised people left after Jesus comes back, whenever it happens. And I'm sorry for them. But—we all make choices. If it's church we want, we can have it. If it's recognition we want, we can find it. But if it's God we want, He'll see to it that we find Him. He looks at our heart and sees what our real desires are. In spite of the garbage, He was, and is, there for me. He will be for you, too.

Thank you again for having the courage to write your book. I'm sure it will be explained away to a lot of devout A.G. people, but there are those of us out there who dare to think for themselves, who are very grateful for some confirmation that perhaps they've been right all along.

Sincerely,

M. P.
former pastor's wife
current lover of God

Whew! Is anybody out there listening? The spunky lady who wrote this letter possesses such a natural gift for writing that she can even make the word "puke" sound charming. A follow-up letter from her, granting me permission to publish her letter, proved to be every bit as informative:

So much has happened in our lives since I wrote you last; let me catch you up briefly.

First of all, as soon as I finished your book, my husband Matthew read it; it took him longer than one day, but not much. I'm happy to say that it has changed his life.

We had a discussion that was very close to a fight, but he finally admitted that he identified very closely with your earlier feelings toward God and the church, and also toward the Assemblies as far as just turning off his own ability to think and letting them think for him. It was very easy for him as well as very flattering for his not-so-good self image. I'm sure he would still be there except for his wonderful wife (ha! ha!).

The result of your book and our discussion was that he took 11 days off and went back and confronted some people about how they affected his marriage and his life. He finally cut the strings binding him to his parents, especially his mother, and headed on to Iowa and the pastor who was the most influential in our lives, and started the whole mess rolling.

After detailing the meeting with that stiff-necked pastor, who denied any responsibility for the problems caused the family, she goes on to say:

> Enough of that. I've read your book again, and loved it more the second time. Our lives have changed never to be the same. I'm glad and VERY GRATEFUL. It must have been very painful for you to expose yourself the way you did. From the bottom of my heart: thank you.
>
> I was very excited when I got your letter. I hoped you would respond, but I never expected a reply so soon. It came while Matthew was gone, so I had time to read it over and think about it quite a bit before I shared it with Matthew.
>
> I give you permission to use my letter and my experience in any way that will help others who are going or have gone through the same thing. I remember how alone and lonely I felt, and how that feeling made me doubt myself and almost accept what they were feeding me as God and truth. If I can be a part of keeping others from doing that and make their hurt and confusion somewhat less, then let's do it.
>
> When I think of all the events that led up to my getting the opportunity to read your book, how much it has helped and changed our lives, the fact that I wrote to you at all and told you things I haven't ever put on paper, let alone receiving a reply, I know that God not only exists, but that He loves us very much and has a purpose for all our lives, even the ugliest part of them.
>
> Thank you very much for your part—you obviously care about PEOPLE very much; it was what I noticed most when I read your book the second time. I'll do whatever I can to help; just let me know what and when.
>
> Cordially,
>
> M. P.

So far, so good.

Here's another spirited lady for the followers of the Assemblies of God to consider. Notice her description of the collection method used by her former church. This "Tribute of Money" idea should have died out with the Middle Ages.

September 23, 1989

Dear Austin Miles:

This is *not* a *hate* letter, but one of empathy and understanding!

Back in '73, my late husband and I left the dearest little community church to attend an Ass. of God church (appropriate title, eh?). We had been "filled with the Spirit" and felt we must. My husband was a choir director and organist.

Upon our joining the Ass. of God church, he formed the first choir the church had had. During the 1½ years we were there he put on two lovely Christmas cantatas, a lovely musical drama and formed a quintet of four high school boys and one girl which performed at various churches in our area. This group included our son, who hated this church from the minute we went there, and still does. He attended out of repsect for us but left the minute he turned 18.

At one point we walked out when the minister insulted my husband, but determined to return after the Christmas programs. (Music to him was like Show Biz to you.)

My hubby, a diabetic with heart trouble, was just fine while we went to the church, but very soon after we left he began to have serious problems. These were so bad that he could not work the last four years of his life. A curse from God?? *NO!* Emotional stress and the heartache of disappointment, not God!

Another thing which strengthened our resolve to leave must be mentioned. The minister got a huge, golden scale. He sat on the plate on one side and told the parishioners emphatically that they must give to their building program until the donations placed on the other side equalled his weight. Ye Gods! These were not well-to-do people at all! (We should have gotten *lots* of pennies to balance it!) (Or maybe slugs!!!)

For a while after we left, my husband had a period of real doubt about the reality of God and the Bible. I didn't because I have always known God is real, but I kept my mouth shut because I loved my husband and wanted him to be comfortable and secure in that love until he died. After a while he again was reading his Bible and when he was up to it we would attend a mainline Protestant church. He died in 1980 three weeks after his 53rd birthday.

I now attend a church (very small) with a pastor who, with his brilliant mind and diligent research into the history of Bible times, and into a knowledge of ancient Greek and Hebrew, has opened up the meaning of many scriptural passages which have been mistranslated, thereby giving a misuse (and excuse) for many incorrect ideas about God. For example, women are *not* second place people in God's eyes. I had always known this anyway, as had my husband, which helped to keep our marriage successful. My good education and good jobs kept us going during his illnesses.

I had no knowledge of your book until our minister held up your book last Sunday, and gave us a brief run-down on it. I borrowed it Thursday night and devoured it! At one point in my reading I thought surely no church could be so evil and still act so "Christian," but as I read on, it all came together. They were more impressed by the FBI than they were with you, even though they *knew* you were a good man!

Your story reminds me of the Old Testament story of Joseph being sold into captivity by his brothers. Who came out the victor? Joseph! Perhaps you are the surgeon who is removing a cancerous growth! At any rate, I can only say, "Thank you," and ask the real true God to bless you!

Sincerely yours,

Mary R. N.
San Bernardino, Calif.

In her response to my request to print her letter, the above correspondent expressed a sentiment shared by most Christians who have written me.

November 30, 1989

Dear Austin Miles,

Your letter arrived while I was on tour in Israel. I hope this response will be in time to be of use to you. You do indeed have my permission to use what I have written. I would prefer, of course, that you use my initials, but if that is not satisfactory, you may use my name. I am certainly looking forward to your new book.

You are doing a great service to all Christians in exposing those who debase the name of Jesus Christ [emphasis mine]. But, believe me, there are many who love Him and worship Him in sincerity and truth.

Most Sincerely,

Mary R. N.

September 28, 1989

Dear Mr. Miles:

I saw you on television talking about your book and immediately went to my local library & put the book on reserve.

Yesterday, I picked it up from the library, and I found it a real "blockbuster." The book is such an eye opener, that I haven't been able to put it down.

Thank God someone like you has the courage to speak frankly about the type of Christians that are part of the Pentecostal Church.

Please continue to speak out because genuine Christians, like myself—are eager to know the truth behind contemporary religion—

Yours Truly,

Sandra S.
Providence, R.I.

August 22, 1989

To: Austin Miles
    San Francisco, California

Via: Prometheus Books
c/o Published Author Dept.
700 East Amherst Street
Buffalo, New York 14215

From: S. W. Waugh
      Oklahoma

I have never tried to contact an author before, but feel I must write Austin Miles . . .

for his courage

He is not alone, there are others of us who can assist in writing sequels to the book *Don't Call Me Brother*. Keep your chin up. I am recommending your book to all I meet as *must* reading.

Please forward my "thumbs up" encouragement. I would call the sequel "Do ya Have A PROBLEM WITH DAT?"

Living next door to a Pentecostal neighbor.

Thank you

S. W. Waugh

In a "permission to print" follow-up letter, this writer added some information with particular significance:

November 15, 1989

Just a note of interest.
    My 82 yr. old Mother, ex-teacher, living in Sr. Ctr. in So. Whitley, Indiana, could not borrow book *Don't Call Me Brother* at Peabody Library in Columbia City, Indiana. She put

a request in while there. This was in September. Just a week ago library called—They now have a copy. Between two dates, I wanted her to have book, purchased another copy which I sent out Oct. 16. To date, eight others within the Sr. complex have read and re-read book. Book became topic for one of their weekly Bible Study sessions. Exciting? You bet it is. Your courage in writing your book is—can't find words. Thanks a million times and do keep your head held high.

God speed, dear friend.

S. W. Waugh

The town mentioned in this letter, Columbia City, Indiana, made national news a few years ago. A little boy desperately needed medical help. His parents, devout members of the Assemblies of God church there, were convinced by that church that God would heal their son. According to church officials, to resort to secular medical assistance would show a "lack of faith." So to "prove their faith" and "to please God," the thoroughly indoctrinated parents refused to take their son to a doctor. The little boy died as a result of his parents' negligence. In a television interview the father was asked, "What does this do to your faith?" The little boy's father, brainwashed into believing that he was still right, thrust his chin out defiantly and said, "Why this just *increases* my faith more than ever!" A pathetic but frightening scene.

In 1987 I stayed overnight in Columbia City. I looked for the name of the infamous church in the directory but couldn't find a listing for it. I asked the desk clerk of the Christian-owned motel where I was staying overnight about the church. She gave me this startling explanation: "Oh, they changed the name of the church because there were so many deaths there."

Now, consider this carefully and with full attention. The familiar name of that cult church was deliberately disguised for the sole purpose of deceiving you and to conceal the truth from the unsuspecting who might be enticed to enter and become involved with this "house of God." The name of that church has been changed again since my visit and probably will be changed again. Just remember, it is an Assemblies of God church.

It is good to hear that *Don't Call Me Brother* has found its way to Columbia City. I am particularly happy that the residents of the Senior Citizen Center are reading it. The elderly are the primary targets of these church leaders since they are the most trusting, least resistant, and most vulnerable—and usually have some money saved.

November 9, 1989

Dear Friend—Thank You,

You have put into words, that which I lack the skills to do. It took me nearly 40 years to finally gain my freedom from "the church" and the ideas of religion. During that 40 years "they" extracted a very great price from me also. Everything I held sacred or of value was taken from me— but that is another story.

I've given a copy of your book (and have another on order for friends to read) to a young niece who married into this family/brotherhood of insanity (as you said, those people are crazy) (more truth than you may have realized). I hope that she and my nephew will read your book and get out of there.

Perhaps others will fall into their trap, but because of your book many more will also gain their freedom.

Hope your Lori will read your exposé and also get out, and IF you or she have not remarried, then perhaps Rose Marie will now see what really happened and how you and she were played against one another, then—who knows? Those of us who like happy outcomes always have hope—

I seldom (if at all) write to anyone who writes books unless they have your courage to name names, with times, dates & places, but I wanted to write to you because your subject "hit home" and I wanted to say thank you—so, THANK YOU—my friend and I hope your life is full of happiness from now on—

With Sincerity,

Dan S.
Okla.

P.S.: Whatever you do—Please DON'T BECOME A MARTYR by allowing this to cause you to hate them, thereby giving them control of you again. As the old saying goes, "You can lead a horse to water but you can't make him drink." Some people do not want to see the truth.

As you will read, many of those who write in response to *Don't Call Me Brother* asked about Rose Marie and Lori, and if there had been any contact or reaction from them since the book was published. I don't know if my daughter ever read my book, since I still have not heard from her. I feel numb inside when I think of her as she once was, the lovely little girl who traveled with me and the circus—who grew up to be a talented musician and beauty queen, but turned her back on everything, including me, when she became a born-again Christian. Several letter-writers have asked about my personal life currently. But more on that later.

The evil connected with the Assemblies of God is not confined to mind control. This shocking letter is one of many I received that relates how rape and death were the rewards for becoming involved with the sect.

September 10, 1989

Dear Mr. Miles:

Thank you for writing the book (*Don't Call Me Brother*). I appreciated your openness, and your honesty about your life and involvement with the Assemblies of God Church. I was given much strength, and my hope renewed from reading your story. For I too am a former Assemblies of God member. I left the church two years ago. I was 28 years old at the time, and had been raised AG all of my life. My life too was a mess when I first left the church, and I had a broken heart. I was lonely, confused, and didn't know where to turn, and in the midst of this I had a friend commit suicide which added all the more pain and pressure to my already broken life. I left my church for several reasons, my decision to leave was something that did not happen just over night. It took a series of built-up events that brought me to a final decision to leave. A youth leader in our church tried to rape my friend's daughter, and this event was passed off like no big deal, or like an everyday occurrence. The church took the youth leader's side, and my friend's daughter ended up being shunned by the people in our church, and my pastor told me if this got out about what happened, everyone would call the girl a whore. I grew furious with my pastor and this church I had grown up in all of my life. I couldn't believe Christians could be like this. Well, my friend's daughter is deeply hurt over this situation, left the church, and is now in counseling. This girl's dad and mom almost lost their marriage over everything, and the girl's brother got an ulcer. The other thing that finally got me to leave our church was when our church's youth pastor became sick with cancer, medical treatment was resisted, and all they did was pray and fast around him 24 hours a day. He died! He was 26 years old, I think, young and I believe could still be here today if the proper treatment would have been given to him in time. He had the type of cancer most people can live with for many years. Well, my stories could go on and on. My life is still very traumatized by my past involvement with the AG, but I am a lot more free now, and at peace. I've had to go through a lot of counseling and therapy. I hope also to be like you, share my story and help others whose lives have been controlled or traumatized by the AG church. Thanks again for sharing your story.

Peace Be With You Now.
Keep Up the Good Work.

Miss C.
Minn.

As always, the reaction from die-hard Assemblies of God members and their clergy to such a report is: "This is just an isolated case and you're using it to paint the entire Assemblies of God with the same brush! You are of the devil! The *majority* of Assemblies of God churches are *wonderful*, with real, dedicated people of God!"

On the contrary! The many letters included here show that such criminal actions are much more common than the Assemblies of God would ever admit.

Notice that in the letter you just read the victim of the attempted rape did not report the incident to the police, nor did her parents, who certainly should have. They rarely do, however, because of the extreme emotional pressure placed on them by the church "to do nothing that would harm the cause of Christ." I have heard that cover-up phrase many times. As a result, these perverted church leaders get away with crimes that other citizens would be severely, and rightfully, punished for committing.

A good case in point took place during the latter part of 1989. A high-profile, prominent, *and trusted* church leader with the Pentecostal Assemblies, the Canadian affiliate of the Assemblies of God, suddenly resigned from his church under suspicious circumstances and disappeared. There were some quiet but guarded rumblings about "sexual indiscretions," even though the board of his church, which is located near Toronto, refused to discuss the issue publicly. Finally, a church spokesperson made this statement to *The Globe and Mail:* "It is nobody's business what happened. The Church is taking care of the matter from within."

Keep in mind that this "man of God," who enjoys a tax-free ride at the public's expense and who is able to reap a personal fortune because of the special privileges that come with his ecclesiastical office, can tell that same public to take a flying leap—that his conduct is none of their business.

I uncovered the following facts about that trusted preacher that have been hidden until now. The first incident involved a minor girl in his church. He molested her. The parents went to the Royal Canadian Mounted Police (RCMP) to make a report. The Pentecostal church leaders exerted such pressure against the family that they withdrew the charges. What's even more outrageous, the police, instead of fulfilling their sworn duty to investigate such charges, pulled back and are now being tight-lipped about the incident. My source for this is in the RCMP in Toronto.

The second incident involved sexual relations with a married woman who had come to this wretched man for counseling. A person is at his or her most vulnerable when seeking counseling. This minister knew how to take full advantage of the situation—and did. What's more, *many of them do,* according to the records I've accumulated. This married pastor not only betrayed the position of trust supposedly given him by God Himself, but he betrayed his entire family as well. As is usual in these cases, this particular minister gives off an aura of such wholesomeness, stability, and trustworthiness that no one would ever have suspected he was capable of such deceit or uncontrollable lusts—the very lusts he preaches against.

In the third incident, the same pastor was stopped by the police for drunk driving. He was let go, without any charges being brought against him.

This pastor's famous brother-in-law, in an attempt to squelch the rumors, stated that what his brother-in-law did "was *not* sin, only silliness." Even the superintendent of the Pentecostal Assemblies gagged over that explanation and fired back, "That was not a case of silliness. What happened was SIN!"

The degenerate pastor is presently in a "counseling center for ministers" in Florida. He should be in jail. As if this were not enough, new revelations have since surfaced regarding on-going homosexual relationships involving this pastor over a period of several years.

It is interesting to note that the pastor who occupied the pulpit of that same church, preceding the one with the famous brother-in-law, also disappeared over a sex scandal. It all came out when a young woman wanting to join the respected church said to the board of directors: "I would like to join, but please have the pastor stop making advances to me." An indignant board member said, "Why, we can't do anything like that without proof." The young woman came back to the board with a tape that had been recorded under her bed during a sex session with the minister, which he had initiated (with what appears to be a willing participant) during one of his house calls. The evidence was irrefutable. The pastor took off. This "minister" is now saving souls (and no doubt bodies) in a church he currently pastors in New Jersey.

Remember, the sexual violations you are reading about, especially those involving children, are only the ones that have been *found out*. Chances are that many, many more such sins have skillfully been swept under the carpet by each of these culprits, leaving in their path a scourge of twisted, broken personalities and lives. And these master deceivers will continue to do it again and again until their brainwashed followers stop protecting them, protect their families instead, and take the necessary action to have these wicked preachers put away for good.

Sex with children and child molestation, prevalent in Satan worship and witches' covens, seem to be every bit as prominent in Assemblies of God and Pentecostal churches, only much more subtle. Here is an eye-opening letter on that subject by one victim.

Prince George, B.C.
Canada
October 30, 1989

Austin Miles
Prometheus Books
700 East Amherst St.
Buffalo, New York 14215
U.S.A.

Dear Mr. Miles:

I have purchased your book and read it with great interest.

I too have been hurt by the church and am now trying to regain my faith outside the church.

I commend you for speaking out and exposing corruption.

What I did find interesting was your admission of being sexually abused.

I believe you would find answers and help if you went for help regarding this issue. I have found many of the answers and even those regarding my faith in this context.

Your trouble with deception, trust, power issues, etc., can be healed in getting help for your sexual abuses.

I'm looking forward to another book published somewhere down the line telling us about how you regained your faith because I can see that you were touched and used by God and I think that can happen again. In fact, I believe he is using you right now in a unique way.

Sincerely,

Mrs. Kathy F.

The subject of sexual abuse seemed to have particular significance for this woman, even though the reason was not too clear. I wrote to ask her permission to print her letter. Her reply included information that pieced it all together in yet another classic story of gross violation of trust by the Christian community.

Prince George, B.C
Canada
November 20, 1989

Dear Mr. Miles,

Today I received your thank-you card in the mail as well as the little note and I sat here and cried. Do you know that the last time I talked to our Pastor (a year ago) and told him I was getting help for my Sexual Abuse he said "Well, that is a Spiritual problem—all you need to do is read your Bible and Pray!! I told him off—I said "Your church (Pentecostal) is the stupidest church I've ever been in and furthermore your sermons are so boring it makes me sick." (He never visits!)

Last Summer I met him in a bookstore and he came slithering up to me and said "We miss you"—I by this time felt stronger so I looked at him and in a non-threatening voice (in fact a little sad) said, "Well I'm sorry to say this but we don't miss you one bit." He never missed a beat and continued with small talk and then slithered away.

I have had 3 years of Bible School training and at the age of 49. I have been in the church ever since I moved from The Homestead into town. I have been in almost every evangelical church there is and I can identify and verify almost everything you have said in your book as it relates to my own experience.

My husband could identify with your wife 100% and now that we have both stopped looking to the church many of our personal struggles have disappeared.

Austin, I still mourn for the dream I always had on The Homestead imagining all that love, etc., etc.

Our family started off by being saved through a radio evangelist and the teaching was much like the TV evangelists.

Now after all these years I have been getting help for the sexual abuse (which often happened in the church as an adult as well). My Mom still won't face up to my abuse and only recently put the blame back on me by saying I should have fought back. She said "I don't want to hear about what happened 30 years ago. I want to talk about The Lord's soon return." (She also was sexually abused, by the way.)

Every day I struggle to find what's right for me in how to find a caring community without having to deny any part of my real life experience. I hope your new book will help me on my journey.

You may use anything I say here in your book if it would help.

Sincerely,

Mrs. Kathy F.

P.S. My husband used to work in the circus in Australia!

Kathy F. enclosed a copy of a story she wrote detailing the experience that scarred her for life.

February 1953—Age 12
"A VISIT"

The thought of a long sleigh ride through the woods was enough to rob me of sleep the night before we left.

At the age of twelve, anything that I could think of, and especially do, heightened my physical awareness of my changing body and the hopes and dreams that come with it.

Dad piled the sleigh-box full of hay and then we heaped on the blankets. Even my Mom showed more interest than she usually did. After all, she would be able to visit another older woman who was more mature in our religious faith. She talked about the love and kindness that she was sure we would receive.

It was fun to watch the horses break a new path in the unmarred snow. Chickadees and bluejays fluttered to safer branches overhead. The snow shone brightly and I almost imagined that we were that happy family I had always dreamed about. If only we had better fellowship, our home life would improve and there wouldn't be so much fighting.

At last we arrived at our destination and it was just as Mom had described. We were welcomed with great warmth and by this time we were grateful to feel the heat and safety of their large and roomy home.

We were so excited about being in that home where there was an upstairs as well as an indoor bathroom. I had never seen so much luxury!

The meals we were served were so generous. How nice to sit down to a full set table—just as I had imagined it to be. Mr. Sutherland was always laughing and joking, and although I wasn't used to a person like that, I thought he was at least happy.

I especially remember Sunday when we all sat down to a feast of chicken and apple pie. I was truly fascinated with so much food and was surprised when I was allowed to eat as much as I pleased.

After we all cleared the table and washed the dishes, we were invited into the living room where Mrs. Sutherland sat herself down to the old pump organ. The music sounded heavenly, and we all joined our voices singing hymns and choruses until we tired of it. Mr. Sutherland seemed to be in fine voice and it almost looked like he was showing off as he stood there as proud as a peacock.

We sat there chatting, and relaxed, and then someone suggested that we all go for a walk.

I was still fascinated with the organ and imagined myself an instant master as the music would flow from my fingertips. With these thoughts in mind, I said I would like to stay behind, so there I was alone, with my fantasies at last to be realized.

I waited to make sure they were truly gone, and then, I got up and began to move cautiously toward the organ. Then I stopped abruptly as I heard footsteps coming back into the house.

Before I had time to think, there stood Mr. Sutherland. In a split second he grabbed me and began to squeeze my breasts and crotch. I remember struggling to escape, and believe I did manage to hide behind the stove.

Just as if a curtain was pulled, my memory is lost from that moment until again I remember sitting in this sleigh waving goodbye.

As we approached home, with the gloom descending upon us, I told my parents about what had happened.

My Dad had a dark look in his face, and stated with great sadness, "We will never go there again." My Mom said nothing.

As I look back now, I realize that both my Mom and Dad used the coping mechanisms that they learned as abused children. That was all that was offered to me. I used those coping skills for a good many years of my life, but now, after 16 months in group therapy and the help of a skilled therapist, I have been given many other options and ways of coping in this life.

As I continue to work on the healing of my inner child, I hope that this clear and full picture of my abuse will fade as an old photograph, and perhaps I will even be able to store it in the attic of my memories where it will no longer shape the journey of my life.

A handwritten note at the bottom of the page explained: "This took place near a little town in Alberta. I left my home and parents as soon as I was old enough."

II

"Blaspheous"

Am I therefore become your enemy, because I tell you the truth?
Galatians 4:16

Not everyone agreed that *Don't Call Me Brother* served a good purpose. In October 1989, the following notice was mass-mailed to the
followers of the late faith healer Rev. William Branham, complete
with instructions to do battle:

Spoken Word Outreach Center
True Vine Memorial Library
P.O. Box 2681
Bartow, Fl 33830 USA
Bro. Duane Dean, Director Ph (813) 665-9398

VERY IMPORTANT—PLEASE READ!

Dear Brothers and Sisters:

Greetings in the name of our Lord Jesus Christ. Enclosed
is a copy of three pages from a new book by Mr. Austin
Miles, a well-known former member of the P.T.L. Club. The
book is called *DON'T CALL ME BROTHER*, published in 1989,
just a few months ago. This book exposes the P.T.L. scandal.
Because of the popular interest in the subject of the P.T.L.
scandal, this book will be read by millions of people all over
the world!

In this book, the author makes false statements about Bro. Wm. Branham. The reason I am writing is to encourage all the people that read this letter to write the publisher of the book and ask him to clear up these lies and false statements.

Address your letter to:

> Prometheus Books
> Attn: Editor of *Don't Call Me Brother*
> 700 East Amherst Street
> Buffalo, NY 14215

or call, Toll Free: [Prometheus toll-free number]

I believe we need to contend for the faith and stand up against the lies that are in this book!

Thank you and God bless you.

> Bro. Duane Dean
> Director
> Enclosure

A total of ten letters poured in as a result of the appeal. The first was addressed directly to Prometheus Books, ATTENTION: Editor.

To whom it may concern:

To my way of thinking, it looks like this world would know by now that God means what He says, with all signs and wonders, and "THUS SAITH THE LORD," spoken through God's prophet William Marrion Branham. Could you even imagine or think wrong, and say such blaspheous [sic] things against not the prophet, but against God. Remember what His own chosen people done to Moses. They murmured and complained about that one man leadership, and dathan and korah [sic] rose up against Moses (really God), and said, "you're not the only Holy one Moses," and God just opened up the earth and swallowed them up, and all who went along with their rottenness. No doubt they made statements that Moses was wrong in all what he said, but if God was speaking through him, that was God doing the speaking, so all that I can say is, "May God have mercy on your soul for making blaspheous [sic] statements against God's prophet, and the tragic thing, against Our Lord Jesus Christ." Remember Jesus told those religious *leaders of His day, you can speak against Me now, but when* the Holy Ghost comes and does the same thing through His Prophet Bro. Branham, it would be unforgiven in this world, and the world to come. Where does that put a person, that has made false erroneous statements against God's prophet?

The first thing that a person should do, is to find out by writing to the prophet's son Billy Paul Branham who traveled with his dad 7 times around the world, and he could tell you if all this rotten gossip about the prophet were true.

I'm a real protestant, and I'm protesting for you or whoever to not put anything about God's prophet in your book unless you know what you're talking about, and if you do, God on the day of judgment will show you right back in your face what you printed, and that it was blaspheous [sic].

Remember what the Lord said, "Many will come to me on that day, and say Lord, have not I cast our devils in your Name, and have we not done many mighty works in your Name," and He will say depart from me you workers of iniquity (something that you know you shouldn't do, and you do it anyway, and something that you know you should do, and you refuse to do it). It isn't the fellow what thought he didn't have a chance to make Heaven, but the disappointment at the judgment will be those that thought they could do anything and make it. Don't put those statements about our prophet, and God's prophet in that book.

A Warriour for
The Lord Jesus Christ

According to the envelope, the "Warriour" who sent the letter on October 20, 1989, was Thomas M. Jordan of Mabscott, West Virginia. He expressed himself in the best way he could, and his comments deserve serious attention.

First of all, there is positively no place in the Bible where Jesus referred to "Bro. Branham" by name, as Mr. Jordan maintains. Nor is it anywhere even remotely suggested in the Holy Scriptures that to speak in an unfavorable manner of William Branham ". . . would be unforgiven in this world, and the world to come."

The *only* unforgivable sin, according to the Bible these deceived people claim to know, is found in St. Matthew 12:31–32: "Wherefore I say unto you, *all* manner of sin and blasphemy shall be forgiven unto men: but the blasphemy against the Holy Ghost shall not be forgiven unto men. And whosoever speaketh a word against the Son of Man, it shall be forgiven him: but whosoever speaketh against the Holy Ghost, it shall not be forgiven him, neither in this world, neither in the world to come."

The term "blasphemy" applies only to something spoken against God (and His Holy Spirit, being part of God), but never to man. The *Funk & Wagnall's Dictionary* defines "blasphemy" as: "Evil or profane speaking of God or sacred things: claiming the attributes of God." I would advise all preachers to pay close attention to the last part of that definition.

As revealed by this letter, we can see that false teaching comes out of the Branham ministry, that it twists the meaning of the Holy Scriptures, encourages the glorification of the man by his followers, and is characterized by a conspicuous lack of formal education. This too is perpetuated by the church of Jesus Christ. To discourage knowledge is to encourage subjugation. To accomplish this purpose, the preachers constantly refer to 1 Corinthians 3:19: "For the wisdom of this world is foolishness with God. For it is written, He taketh the wise in their own craftiness."

The preachers also convince us that "the mysteries of the Bible" can only be unraveled by them, "as the Holy Spirit directs." This is the basis for the church's manipulation of its followers and ultimately its path to power. *This* is blasphemy.

October 14, 1989

To the Author of *Don't Call Me Brother:*

I want to write and tell you that you have been misinformed about Br. William Branham. He did not use the old envelope trick you knew about—he was a prophet of God. And God told him those things—probably why you got sick is because the man lied about the prophet of God—he didn't die in a flood either. You are Walking dangerously. You need to Check this out & Correct your mistakes.

Louise Holden
Newland, N.C.

You should read "A Man Sent from God" and learn the real truth about W. M. Branham. He is a prophet for the end time but only The Bride of Jesus Christ can see the truth.

Beckley, W.Va.
November 17, 1989

Prometheus Books
700 East Amherst St.
Buffalo, N.Y. 14215

Attn.: Editor

Dear Sir:

I was very disappointed to learn your company has published a book that has told such outrageous lies as was told on Rev. William Branham. I am referring to the publication *Don't Call Me Brother*. The facts are this:

1. Bro. Branham did not at any time have in his possession the prayer cards that the individuals had written their sickness, needs, etc., on.

2. This brother also refers to the "trick" used by others that he had been told about, in "planting" a person in the audience. I personally know many people who were prayed for in Rev. Branham's meetings who were total strangers to him, yet Rev. Branham, through a divine gift God placed in his life, told them their needs, prayed for them, and pronounced them healed. We know many who had fatal diseases and illnesses and would have died many years ago had God not healed them.

3. I suppose these accusations are to be expected. After all, the people in Jesus' day accused Him of casting out sicknesses and evils "by the power of Satan." I suppose these false accusers are the offspring of this same group.

I certainly hope you will reconsider publishing this controversial book.

Sincerely,

Mr. & Mrs. Charles Gravley

One must question why it would have been necessary for individuals seeking prayer to write down their sickness, needs, etc., if indeed God Himself "told them their needs" through His "prophet" Brother Branham. Did God need a cue card in order to impart this "divine revelation"?

As pointed out in this letter, most of the people in the audience were strangers to Rev. Branham. Yet he revealed intimate details of their lives as they came forward to "be healed." What Rev. Branham revealed corresponded perfectly with what had been written on each of these person's prayer cards. As witnessed by his audiences, the evangelist seemingly did not touch or see the prayer cards. And so they were convinced that what they had witnessed was a "supernatural gift" in operation. Equally amazing is the fact that in the version I know *one person* planted in the audience sets the entire incredible performance in motion.

I demonstrated this trick on "The Shirley Show" on CTV in Toronto during the latter part of 1989. Associates of Rev. David Mainse of the Christian TV program "100 Huntley Street," along with evangelicals in the studio audience, did everything possible, short of starting a riot, to prevent me from exposing the con that generates millions of dollars in donations. How the envelope trick works is fully explained in *Don't Call Me Brother*, pages 159–160.

Minot, N. Dak.
November 1, 1989

Dear Sir:

It appears from your writing that you are believing some hearsay. You are far too late to dispute William Marrion Branham's Ministry. I was having gall-bladder trouble in 1951 and my husband had incurable Malaria. I heard he was coming to Minneapolis, Minnesota, where we were living at the time. We went to the Meeting and I was given card No. 3—my husband did not want a card, but sat way back in the hall, when my No. was called an usher took the card to keep order, Mr. Branham didn't see the card. He said to me you are a Missionary for I see the Ocean waves all around you now you go to the Jews as I see the black skulled [sic] caps all around you, you have a pain in the pit of your stomach but it comes from gall-bladder trouble, you are not up here for yourself only there sits a man almost bald-headed why its your husband he has Malaria very badly from being in Africa years and years, Thus sayeth the LORD be thou whole both of you. We were instantly healed both of us.

In 1963 my husband dropped dead after the service (I had been a Registered Nurse 34 years already). I called for Mr. Branham and he came to where Edmund was lying on the floor and prayed over him and instantly he came back to life.

Write to:

The Voice of God Recordings, Inc.
P.O. Box 950
555 E. 10th Street
Jeffersonville, Indiana 47131

They can give you Books and Tapes. Vindicated and manifested.

Yours sincerely,

Ruth Way

Notice that the woman coming to this "man of God" seeking prayer and healing ". . . was given card no. 3." Again, why would an identifying numbered card with personal information on it be required when, as it is suggested, *God will reveal everything* about that person through His prophet? Isn't it astonishing that the workings of God would be tied to such details? The writer of the letter went on to describe how the usher took the numbered card and that ". . . Mr. Branham didn't see the card." I have heard this exact description of a magician's performance.

According to her testimony, Mrs. Way's husband did not want a card, yet Rev. Branham revealed his needs, too. During my ten years as an evangelist I saw many such requests. It seems obvious to me that the woman, desperate for her husband's healing, included that information on her prayer card, thus supplying Rev. Branham with everything he needed to perform two "miracles."

Tragically, people who blindly follow such a "faith ministry" will never accept the truth. They would rather continue living in their own fantasy world, no matter what it costs them.

This next letter, dated November 14, 1989, intrigued me before I opened it. The imprint of a rubber stamp made up in old English-style large letters identified the sender of the communiqué as Rev. Shawn D. Wells of Bradenton, Florida.

Dear Sir,

Greetings in the name of our Lord and Saviour, Jesus Christ.

I am writing to you in regard to a book entitled *Don't Call Me Brother* by Austin Miles.

On page 158, the method of healing stated was quite erroneous. You make William Branham sound as if he were Johnny Carson. William Branham's ministry has never and will never see an equal as has been vindicated by history alone. Page 159 (first paragraph) had a misconstrued meaning of what actually happened during the meeting and on page 160, the Winter Flood being referred to occurred in 1933 and it was in Indiana not Kentucky. William Branham passed this life 12/24/65. Although some people were expecting him to resurrect, I adjure you to say that these were NOT his followers BUT rather fanatics. If any kind of research for this would have been done (even loosely) you could not have

gotten facts so construed into the fantasy of some slanderous devil who prints hearsay without research. I am a close
friend of the Branham family and I will be sending xerox
copies of this to their family, so don't be surprised if you
hear from them.

Rev. Shawn D. Wells

I dropped a letter to Rev. Wells identifying myself as the "slanderous
devil" he had complained to my publisher about. I wrote that I was
willing to publicly correct any possible misconception about Rev.
William Branham that may have been formed by my book. I also
asked and received his permission to print his letter "to set the record
straight."

I want to point out that Rev. Wells is incorrect in stating that
the flood I referred to occurred in 1933. That flood, for which there
are many records, occurred in 1937. Rev. Wells also states in his
letter that the flood "was in Indiana not Kentucky." One has only
to look at a map to see that Kentucky is on one side of the Ohio
River and Indiana is on the opposite side. It would take a real miracle
for that river to spill over just one side. Records will show that
both Kentucky and Indiana suffered severe damage as a result of
that flood. This just shows how reliable and accurate the information
is that comes from the representatives of the William Branham
ministry.

In his reply to my sincere and polite letter, Rev. Wells draws
a comparison between me and Hitler, Mussolini, and Stalin!

Dear Mr. Austin:

I am writing again in response to your letter in which you
wrote to me Nov. 27, 1989. Thank you for your response,
and do know that when I addressed the "slanderous devil"
as you referred to, I referred to a spirit, and not to an individual. The same can be said of Hitler, Mussolini, and Stalin.
Those were instruments yielded to the god of the evil age.
I wanted you to know that the majority of negative things
that are said about Rev. William Branham are here say [sic].
Here say [sic] is not that far off even in spelling of heresy,
it only lacks one vowel. If you want to know the truth of

the man sent from God, well over 400 of his sermons are available in book form and around 1500 tapes in cassette and reel to reel are available. People such as Ern Baxter, Roberts Liardon in particular, have always given their expert advice on William Branham when Liardon never even met William Branham. He gets all his information from second-handed people who were only passing acquaintances who knew no more of Bro. Branham than you know of me. But to be an expert on William Branham brings some kind of self inoculated esteem to different groups of people because some people (like Kenneth Hagin) have testified that Bro. Branham was a prophet of God—but these people never knew the man. He left behind him a legacy and if we are to know anything, let's take what William Branham was by his words and not the words of people who have never met him. And in your case, you printed the word of a heresay [sic] and never even followed up to see if the lie Bedzyk told you was truth or not. If your heart is right and you want to make your wrong right in accordance to the Bible, pull your book off the bookshelves and rewrite it based upon fact and not fiction.

Sincerely,

Rev. Shawn D. Wells
Matt. 10:41

As you can see, Rev. Wells sternly castigated me for printing "here say." Then he knowingly attempted to mislead me and my readers regarding Ern Baxter. Rev. W. J. Ern Baxter was closely associated with William Branham for seven years as Branham's business manager. In that time, he became increasingly disturbed over the message William Branham preached. Today he discourages people from becoming involved with that ministry because of its "false teaching."

I looked up the Scripture verse that Rev. Wells included in which Jesus says: "He that receiveth a prophet in the name of a prophet shall receive a prophet's reward; and he that receiveth a righteous man in the name of a righteous man shall receive a righteous man's reward." I'll do my best.

A personal letter dated December 11, 1989, came by certified mail. The sender, Brother Duane Dean of Spoken Word Outreach Center, had earlier sent out a mass mailing to the followers of the late William Branham in an effort to stir up a harassment letter-writing campaign to my publisher.

Dear Mr. Miles:

Just a note to tell you that you do not have the *facts about Bro. Wm. Branham Right*—He did not used a *card trick* or did He Died in a *Winter flood*. I have many Witness that No *Card Trick* was used, this is a lie and it need to Be *clear up*—if you like I have *Video Tape* and *cassette Tapes of Wm. Branham* and *you will see there are No Tricks, like many of the false charismatic Big Name preacher—We ask you to please* look *into clearing up this matter.*

You may Write or call me and We can clear up this matter and these lies. Bro. Branham was a True man of God that stand against this *false Charismatic Movement* and all these false liar preachers, that Now on T.V.—these preachers like Oral Robert hated Wm. Branham Because he *preach against their sins*. Please let me send you some Tapes of Wm. Branham (Free). I think you *will see,* that this *Man was one of the few, that stand* up for *Truth* and Not this *charismatic Junk.* God Bless.

Bro. Duane Dean

Printed at the bottom of his stationery is a quote: "The Spoken Word is The Original Seed." Bro. Dean included some informative printed material about William Branham in the envelope along with a tract. The tract was consistent with all the others sent to me by Branham followers. It glorified William Branham more than Jesus, and indeed suggested that William Branham might have been Christ in disguise.

The devoted followers of Rev. William Branham are unanimous in their belief that every prophecy and every prediction made by him "came to pass." The definition of a prophet is given on page four of the tract sent to me:

How can we find this true prophet-messenger amidst the multitude of false prophets that swarm the earth today?

For one, God said: "And if thou say in thine heart, how shall we know the Word which the Lord hath not spoken? When a prophet speaketh in the name of the Lord, if the thing follow not, nor come to pass, that is the thing which the Lord hath not spoken, but the prophet hath spoken it presumptuously: thou shalt not be afraid of him" (Dt. 18:21–22). Thus, the way to tell a true prophet is simple: everything he prophesied will come to pass, for God doesn't make any mistakes.

In the same envelope, a glaring contradiction stood out in a copy of a story published in *Arizona Magazine* dated March 26, 1967. The story stated that on February 28, 1963, "Mr. Branham predicted Christ would return to earth around 1977 to claim his bride, that is, the elect or hard core of Christian believers." To the best of my knowledge, William Branham's prophecy did not come to pass. It is now 1990 and we are all still here.

October 20, 1989

Dear Sirs:

In reference to a book titled *Don't Call Me Brother*, pages 158, 159, 160.

There are many serious errors concerning Bro. Branham. I was in Bro. Branham's meetings in Phoenix 1963 & gave my heart to God as a result of his ministry. I have been in many, many of his meetings in Az. & Calif. Also since his auto accident, *not* in a winter flood as your book says, in which he was killed (1965). I have heard & studied many of the aprox. 1100 tapes & books. Also there are 2 films of Br. Branham that show how he conducted his services.

Never have I seen, or anyone I know (100's) of seen, or heard of Bro. Branham conducting any service as described in your book. First of all he did not die as stated. Secondly he *never* told God what to do. Thirdly he ministered around the world (7 times) in many different languages & had to use interpreters & could only read English (7th grade education).

He was the most humble, honest, and Godly man to

walk in shoe leather since Jesus Christ.

I believe you should delete this portion from this book or correct it. I can not believe things like this can be printed without being checked out first. It causes one to doubt anything coming from Prometheus Books. Sorry, but I could not let this go by without Writing.

A Concerned Christian.

Michael H. Johnson
Laveen, Ariz.

November 29, 1989

I am writing this letter in defense of Brother William Marrion Branham. I am personally acquainted with men who are alive today who walked, talked, hunted and fished with Brother Branham. They tell of the many miracles that followed his ministry and everyday life. He never bragged or boasted of himself, but always gave the glory and credit to Jesus Christ. He could have been a very wealthy man. He had many offers. When he left this world his total worth of material possessions and all was five thousand dollars. He had nothing to gain by being deceitful or playing envelope tricks. Because of the gospel that he has preached, my entire family has come to know the Lord Jesus. I, myself, was a drug addict and a hippy. But because God could get one man in His hand in this last day, who would not turn to the right or left or compromise with the Word of God, my life has been changed.

As you know, there are seven church ages. We are living in the last one (Laodicia) and he was the seventh angel or messenger to this church age. He is spoken of in Revelation 10:7, Malachi 4:5, 6, Luke 17:30.

In Zechariah 9:9 it tells of Jesus coming on a foal of an ass. This was fulfilled in Matthew 21:4–5. Why couldn't the Pharisees and Sadducees see it? They had passed the scrolls down for years and years and were great religious men, but they called Him a devil. God always vindicates His Word by making a promise and bringing it to pass. God promised in Malachi that He would send Elijah the prophet and he would turn the hearts of the children back to the faith of the pentecostal fathers. This is not speaking of John the Baptist because the world did not burn after John's message. It is ready for the burning now. It would take me pages to explain his ministry to you, but you cannot see it without a revelation (Matthew 16:17).

Brother Samuel G. Wyco
Beaver, W.Va.

It is impressive that all of the disciples of William Branham are convinced that the Scripture verses they point me to refer directly to the coming of William Branham. The writer of the above letter goes so far as to identify him as "the seventh angel or messenger to this church age." As for his "life being changed" by the ministry of William Branham, Brother Wyco appears to have simply swapped one addiction for another. I must concede that this one appears to be the better of the two.

Mesa, Ariz.
December 12, 1989

Dear Mr. Miles:

You don't want to be called Brother, but may I call you friend?

I hope you won't mind me taking the liberty of writing to you after reading your book *Don't Call Me Brother*.

You have probably received so many letters, some good, some bad, some even worse than bad, that more than likely as each batch comes in, you are probably tempted to throw them in the garbage—unread!

I do hope you will bear with me, however, and that this letter will not meet that fate. I will try to be as brief as possible.

I felt very badly for you when you said you lost God in church. Has it not occurred to you my friend that God was not in that apostate church. God was in you. You did not leave Him behind, as He was not there to begin with.

The scripture bears this out in Rev. 3:14–19 (too much to quote) but those of this last age, God said they were naked and didn't even know it. If they were naked, they obviously were not clothed with His righteousness, therefore they were not His. (They professed to be, of course, but anyone can profess anything.)

Sounds to me in reading verse 17, that you and God saw totally eye to eye concerning them, quote, "You say, I am rich, and increased with goods, and have need of nothing; and know not that you are wretched, and miserable, and poor and blind, and naked."

What actually happened to you my friend is simply that you got unwittingly involved with what Rev. speaks of as the Great Whore and her Harlot Daughters, or as you mentioned in your book, "that falling away" of that apostate church.

What you saw and experienced first hand was the actual fulfillment of that scripture. It should come as no surprise to you that scripture does come to pass.

In Matt. 7:22 Jesus spoke of these when He said, "Many will say to me in that day, Lord, Lord, have we not prophesied in thy name? and in thy name have cast out devils? and in thy name done many wonderful works? And then I will profess to them, I never knew you, depart from me ye that work iniquity."

I feel so very sorry that though you saw the false, you were unable to find the true. As you would certainly know there has to be a true before there can be a false, there has to be a real before there can be an imitation, there has to be a real dollar before there can be a counterfeit. So what you saw, only proves there is a real somewhere.

I sense in your book that you are a very honest, earnest, sincere person with a great deal of intestinal fortitude. Because of this, may I present one more thing to you for your perusal? May I ask you to be as diligent one more time in your search for truth as you have been in the past? May I ask you to hear me out and then truly investigate (not by hearsay), but truly investigate what I have to say to you?

I wish to bring your attention to pages 158, 159, and 160 in your book referring to Rev. William Branham. It appears to me that you took the words and opinion of a man with whom you admit you were not impressed, took his opinion and his story for gospel truth, then put your own interpretation to what he said and immediately came up with the idea that William Branham too was a charlatan.

I have no idea where this Pastor Bedzyk got his information about the letters that Rev. Branham was supposed to have had on the pulpit. I have talked to a number of people who were in many, many of his meetings and they tell me that they never saw him with any letters or even any prayer cards in his hands.

One gentleman told me that Rev. Branham's son Billy Paul would shuffle and shuffle even the prayer cards before handing them out to people, so that the 1-100 A's would be all mixed with 1-100 B's, etc. No one knew, not even Billy Paul, what numbers that Rev. B. would call for. All the prayer card did was get people in the prayer line. Hundreds of times Rev. Branham picked people out of the audience and told them their name, address, and ailment. I suppose one could believe they were "planted," if one wanted to, but seems to me to "plant" hundreds of people in audiences around the world would be quite a drag. In any case, I am enclosing a folder telling of some of the things that occurred in Rev. Branham's life, and I suggest that a man who had God doing the things that God did for him, does not need to use cheap magician tricks.

I am enclosing the names and addresses of some of the people who were in many of Rev. Branham's meetings. May I suggest that you contact them and I trust you will listen to them with an open mind.

Under separate cover, I am sending you a book written by a man who was an eyewitness to much of William Branham's life and also of his death.

I'm not sure where you got the information about Rev. Branham's death, but unfortunately it was totally unreliable information. He did not die in Indiana, nor did he die in a flood. He was critically injured in a car accident (see enclosed picture) six miles west of Freona, Texas, Dec. 18, 1965. He died in a Texas hospital, Dec. 24, 1965.

Also you stated that his body was kept for four months

because his followers expected him to raise from the dead. No doubt some of them did expect it, but I heard his own son say that the reason his body was kept for that length of time was so Rev. Branham's wife, Meda, could recuperate from her serious injuries and then make the decision as to where Rev. Branham would be buried. (They had lived in both Jeffersonville, Indiana, and Tucson, Ariz. His first wife was buried in Jeffersonville.) When Meda was well enough she made the decision and he too was buried in Jeffersonville.

Another of the statements in your book was on page 159 of Rev. Branham yelling with great anger, etc., at the two men who were trying to fool him. I asked the men who knew him well, if they had ever heard him speak in anger, and they said no—they had never heard him even speak as if in frustration.

I never saw the man (except on video) but I have heard many of his taped messages and have heard him refer many times to that incident, *but I have never heard anything that even approached* anger [emphasis mine]. I hope to find the tape of that particular meeting, if I can I will send it to you and you can hear it for yourself and lay another false statement to rest.

From what I have heard and seen and researched, I believe that William Branham portrayed Christ more than any other person in this age. However, lying tongues have done their best to destroy his credibility as they did yours. Since you have been the victim of them, I know you would not want to spread false things about anyone else. This is why I bring these things to your attention. Since your book is widely read I do not know if these things can be corrected, but hopefully, you at least will know the truth.

If you wished to scripturally understand all the things that happened to you in the so-called Christian world, may I respectfully suggest that you would find the answers by listening to some of Rev. Branham's messages, *where he screamed out against such* as that [emphasis mine]—tapes such as The Great Harlot, Jezebel Religion, The First Seal and many others. If you are interested, these are available from The Voice of God Recordings, Inc., Box 950, Jeffersonville, Ind. 47131.

You said that you lost God in church, but that you

might find Him outside the church, and I'm sure you will because that is where He is. Rev. 3:20 says He is outside the church knocking to get back in. However, He knows the "apostate church" won't let Him in, but He says "if any man" will hear my voice and open the door I will sup with him and he with me!

I can't help but earnestly pray that you might be that man, and that the two of you might truly, once again, "sup" together.

Goodbye, my friend, and if for any reason you would want to contact me (even if just to "chew" me out) I would be very pleased to hear from you. Forgive me if I say "God bless you richly, and restore to you all that the canker worm hath eaten."

Very sincerely,

Grace Sawyer

A respected Assemblies of God minister, Reverend John Bedzyk, pastor of Pentecostal Tabernacle in Elmira, New York, gave me the information that is being challenged so vigorously by Branham devotees. A great admirer of William Branham, Pastor Bedzyk would never do anything to discredit his memory. This is made clear in *Don't Call Me Brother*. He did, however, unintentionally tip me off to something I found of interest, having once been a magician.

The method of organizing the information gathered from the audience that Pastor Bedzyk described is positively verified in their letters by the very people who state that "this is false information." If there was no trickery, then why, as pointed out in this letter, would Rev. Branham's son Billy Paul stand in front of the audience and make a special point to "shuffle and shuffle" all the information cards to *prove* there was no trickery? Truth should stand on its own.

Ms. Sawyer politely takes exception to the description of Rev. Branham "yelling with great anger" at the two young men who were trying to fool him. Claiming that people who knew him well never heard him speak in anger, "or even as if in frustration," Ms. Sawyer writes: ". . . I have never heard anything [from Rev. Branham] that even approached anger." She scolded me for "making a false statement." Then, on the same page, Ms. Sawyer advises: ". . . you would find the answers by listening to some of Rev. Branham's messages, where *he screamed out against such as that. . . .*" No wonder Christians end up talking to themselves.

The followers of William Branham were correct in taking me to task for printing incorrect information regarding the prophet's death. Rev. Branham did not die in a flood, as I had been led to believe by Pastor Bedzyk, but as the result of a horrible car crash on December 18, 1965. He had been hit head-on by a young man with a history of trouble. Reverend Branham died from the injuries on Christmas Eve, six days later.

The aforesaid flood, known as the '37 Flood, took a tragic toll on Rev. Branham's life. Both his first wife and his daughter died as the result of a disease contracted during that disaster. It is fairly understandable how these devastating events could have been intermingled in the later telling of the story.

Reverend Bedzyk gave me the information in good faith. I have sorely learned since that dreadful time in my life to "try the spirits" a dozen different ways and then research the matter some more before relying upon any information that comes from Assemblies of God folk. Too often their words are more "gossip-el" than gospel. In any case, I believe everyone *will* agree that Brother Branham is dead, which was the point of that particular story.

The book that Ms. Sawyer sent to me is entitled *The Acts of the Prophet.* The famous photograph that shows a ring of light over Rev. Branham's head dominates the cover. The author, Pearry Green, had been a close friend and confidant of the man that has become a puzzle to me.

The Rev. Branham I read about in this book impressed me in many ways. Some spectacular healings reportedly occurred during his unusual ministry. There appears to be considerable documentation to verify them. Even though born and raised in abject poverty, Rev. Branham showed no interest in money. Further research on my part has shown that no personal scandal has ever been connected with him.

While I harbor certain suspicions about the prayer cards, too many individuals who attended his meetings have refuted the idea that the information was organized in the manner which Pastor Bedzyk described. Latter-day preachers have indeed used the envelope trick and other devices to fleece the flock, but I am now convinced that Rev. Branham did not.

His sincerity in what he did can not be disputed. He did not appear to seek fame for the sake of fame, nor did he try to merchandise God. He exhibited a genuine concern for the afflicted, praying with them for hours in long prayer lines.

With a fervent devotion to his work, Rev. Branham never compromised his beliefs or his position. He once refused to accept a donation of more than a million dollars from a man in Chicago. He wanted to focus his attention on God only, with no distractions. It is easy to see why his followers are still fiercely loyal to him.

The widespread belief that Rev. Branham was divine was subtly encouraged by the evangelist himself. In his book on the church ages, Rev. Branham wrote that there would be some who would worship him, and believe him to be the Messiah, then humbly instructed his audience not to believe it. Nothing fosters an idea more effectively than to bring it up and then elaborately deny it. This is a common public relations maneuver to propel an idea into motion. Rev. Branham then told his followers: "I need no greater place of honor than that which John the Baptist had."

Venerated as he was by his followers, it should come as no surprise that they thoroughly expected Rev. Branham to conquer the untimely death that overtook him. In a vivid account of the events following the fatal accident, Pearry Green tells of accompanying Rev. Branham's body back to Indiana:

> We deplaned at St. Louis, the prophet's body and I, for a layover period until the proper type of aircraft would be available to continue the journey. I never left the side of the casket, even as it was wheeled out across the vast airport to a warehouse. It was in this warehouse that I was to take up a vigil of six hours, with my ear pressed to the casket. Each moment, I expected to hear that prophet say, "Brother Green, get me out of here." It was cold and lonely in that warehouse. Thoughts raced through my mind, questions, more questions. . . . now what?
>
> Again the faithful Word came to my rescue: "Though one rise from the dead, they would not believe." After all, what would I do if he were to speak to me? Would anyone believe me if he did arise? Would Brother Billy Paul believe me? Would Brother Borders? Or would they all blame me

if the body was to turn up missing? At that time, I felt to ask the Lord whether I was being shown that he was to come forth with all the dead in Christ. Then I said, "Lord, don't let him rise here with just me. Wait until there are witnesses." (*The Acts of the Prophet*, p. 174)

Rev. Green tells how he had the casket opened periodically during the trip to make sure the prophet was still inside. "What would have been the furor if I had arrived in Jeffersonville with an empty casket?"

The funeral service took place in Jeffersonville on December 29. According to Rev. Green: "At 4 o'clock, outside after the service, many people began to notice a strange coloration and circles around the sun. My father directed my attention to this unusual dispaly, then left to phone my sisters in Texas to see if the same phenomenon was happening there. He phoned California and other places. Everywhere the answer was the same; the same manifestation was being seen." It had to be a sign from God.

Instead of burying Rev. Branham after the funeral service, his followers took the body back to the funeral home, where it remained in a private upstairs room for four months. During that time, the rumor that William Branham would rise from the dead filtered out of his church and into the community. This telephone conversation on the night before Easter 1966, between a UPI reporter and Rev. Green, is recorded in his book. Rev. Green had just asked the identity of his caller.

"This is Mr. Brown of the United Press International, Louisville," he answered, then abruptly asked, "Aren't you people expecting William Branham to rise on Easter morning?"

The bluntness of his question shook me a little, but I managed a careful answer, "Well, sir, there may be some that believe that. What faith are you?"

"Baptist," came the reply.

"Don't you believe in the resurrection?" I countered. "Don't you believe in the second coming of the Lord?"

"Yes, sir," he admitted.

"Well, so do we," I said.

His next question was designed to put words in my mouth.

"Do you think it could take place in the morning?"

"Sir," I said innocently, "I wouldn't be a bit surprised when it would happen."

The vague answers that Rev. Green gave to the UPI reporter would give the followers of Rev. Branham an "out" in case things didn't work out as they hoped. However, the events leading up to that Easter Sunday morning show quite clearly that the supporters of William Branham fully expected that he would rise from the dead. Today, these same people, including the writer of the book quoted above, staunchly deny that such a miracle was expected.

The Acts of the Prophet is filled with wild stories of bizarre visions and strange prophecies that would bust a gut to swallow. The most incredible of the prophesies is found on page 118. During 1959 Brother Branham plugged into Heaven to receive and proclaim this word for our edification: "Thus saith the Lord, someday Russia will drop an atomic bomb on the Vatican and in one hour she will be destroyed." This would seem to be a rather elaborate procedure by which to eliminate the Vatican, no matter how many feathers it ruffled. And in slow motion yet!

Standing in front of The May Company in downtown Los Angeles in 1965, Rev. Branham made this prophetic statement to his son: "Billy, I may not be here, but you won't be an old man until sharks swim right where we are standing."

To his California audiences, Rev. Branham thundered: "Thus saith the Lord, the city of Los Angeles, as the result of an earthquake, will break off and slide off into the Pacific Ocean." His message so rattled his followers who lived there that they frantically asked his advice on what they should do. Rev. Branham said: "I want you brothers to know this, that if you have any friends or relatives in Los Angeles, if I were you, I'd get them out as quickly as possible." Many uprooted their families, sold their homes, quit their jobs, and fled. Some moved close to their esteemed leader's home in Tucson, Arizona.

It is sobering to observe that this "prophecy," given in God's name, which confused, frightened, and unsettled so many people, was spoken exactly twelve days before the life of the man who spoke it was cut short in a bizarre automobile crash.

The William Branham Evangelistic Association is still active today, with a scattering of small churches throughout the United

States and Canada. I am sorry to say that this ministry shares too many of the characteristics of a cult. One of the letter writers advised me to judge William Branham "by his words, not the words of others." This proved to be excellent advice. Here are the words of William Branham in a sermon on marriage and divorce delivered on February 21, 1965, at Parkview Junior High School in Jeffersonville, Indiana, concerning Adam, Eve, and Original Sin:

> The apple that she was supposed to eat, for it's not even Scriptural, now they claim it was an apricot; it was neither one. *She committed adultery*, that brought forth the first child, which was Cain.

In that same sermon, the prophet spoke these words:

> Now I'm speaking to our followers only, *who is following me* and this message only, not the outside. Bear me record of this before God. Just to this group only!

I have found many such examples of false teaching coming out of the William Branham ministry. It has been my understanding that God wants his message shared with the world, not just a select group of people. The emphasis on *"following me"* comes up often in the teachings of William Branham, which again is contrary to the Bible, which tells us to follow Christ. There is entirely too much emphasis placed on the leader.

Regarding his prophesies:

> The Lord has let me foresee things, tell things that have happened, will happen, are happening, and not one time has it ever failed, in the tens of thousands of times. Everything that He said would happen, happened.

There are four of his prophesies in this chapter that have so far failed to come to pass. I am certain that research would turn up many more. I greatly respect William Branham as the individual I found him to be during my research. I could not respect him as a Bible teacher, however.

Even if I could find more to commend his ministry, the letter from Rev. Branham's son, Billy Paul, would for me seriously challenge the validity of their operation. There is something very revealing in the letter.

Story after story is told and written about the phenomenal light that supernaturally manifested itself around Rev. Branham. The suggestion was that this was a sublime occurrence, a sign of God's endorsement of Brother Branham. But if one looks closely at the photo of Rev. Branham in the lower right-hand corner and the "heavenly light" around his head, you can see that this "divine glow" is silver paint splashed on the wall behind Rev. Branham's head to give that illusion.

This is hardly different from Dr. Robert H. Schuller faking the photograph of him supposedly standing by the Great Wall of China.

October 12, 1989

Mr. Austin Miles

Dear Mr. Miles:

I was amazed after reading your book on *Don't Call Me Brother*. I wonder how much of this or if any of this is true at all, after all the falsehood you spoke of Rev. Branham in your book. How could a man write such awful lies and never check his information any better. No wonder you got sick and had to go to your hotel room after hearing Pastor Bedzyk.

Brother Branham never done "ANY" of these things that you said, and never had an envelope trick, etc., done like you said. He was truly God's Prophet to this age of our day. He was truly a man sent from God, and I would imagine you will be hearing from people around the world to your lies, and I don't know what else will be done in the natural as you "printed" falsehoods on him.

Where did you get your information of Brother Branham being killed in a great flood in Louisville, Ky. in 1965?

Even a "child" trying to write his first paper in school to make a report would have better facts than this to give to his teacher, than you have that is supposed to be a writer.

So I will leave you with this one thought for you to ponder over. The written Word of God says "Touch not mine anointed, and do my prophets no harm." Now ask yourself this question, "If I lied about all this, and never checked out these statements, and I now have been proved to have lied about this man, and now what if he was a Prophet of God, what have I done, and where does that place me in the eyes of God?" I think your other sickness would be mild to this.

Sincerely,

W. P. Branham

III

God Healed My Cancer (?)

Now faith is the substance of things hoped for, the evidence of things not seen.

Hebrews 11:1

The date of September 11, 1989, will forever be etched in my memory as a chilling admonition never, *never* again allow *anyone* to lead me down the path of blind faith. By surrendering my common sense to these convincing Christian leaders, I almost lost my life. This grand finale, which took place after the publication of *Don't Call Me Brother*, truly completed this man's adventure in born-again Christianity.

Along with the dramatic events of that day, *People Magazine* came out with a story about me and my book. A letter, tucked in an envelope marked "PERSONAL," began its journey to me the next day. The writer, a former acquaintance, had no idea that her letter would arrive at the time of my greatest battle. With uncanny timing, this letter summed up precisely the events which had led me to that fateful day and week in September.

September 12, 1989

Dear Mr. Miles:

You probably won't remember me, but I remember you very well, and couldn't resist writing after seeing this week's issue of PEOPLE magazine.

When you were serving as ringmaster for the Lipizzan Stallion Show, you came to Duluth, Minnesota. It was 1972 or 1973, and I was the public relations account executive assigned to accompany you to local media outlets to promote the show. You may remember that I also invited you to a performance of Sweet Adelines in which my mother was singing, and gave you a little blue musical note as a keepsake of that singularly unimportant night.

I remember that we spent considerable time talking, not only between media appearances but also at dinner and late into the evening over pizza. We talked mostly about religion; I was expressing my doubts about "organized religion"; I had had a couple of negative exposures to "church," and considered myself to be, if not an agnostic, at least a skeptic. You listened with great sensitivity and compassion, and shared many of your own feelings about your faith, which as I recall had been greatly strengthened by your experience with a serious illness from which you hadn't been expecting to recover (am I right?? It's been nearly eighteen years!). I left with the feeling that at least one person who was "into religion" was into it for the right reasons, and had his value system very much under control. In today's jargon, I thought you were "self-actualized."

As I read the story about the Bakkers, I couldn't help remembering our conversations. It must have been terribly disillusioning for someone of your sincerity and conviction to see such hypocrisy in action. We all recognize the humanity and the fallibility of people like Jim Bakker. However, the abuse of his power over the vulnerable is something for which there is no excuse. People who really care about other people could not do such things, especially over the long term as the Bakkers did.

It is the mark of the impact our brief encounter had on me that all these years later, I felt disappointed when I learned that you had been a part of Bakker's organization, and greatly relieved when I read further, to find that you had left PTL when you understood the reality of the Bakkers' operations. Somehow, I could never have associated you with such a violation of people's trust.

It was fun to read about your book (isn't this at least

your second?). I've ordered a copy from an area bookstore, and I look forward to reading it and re-meeting you through its pages. The trail from the stallion show to the PTL Club is a fascinating one, I'm sure.

If circumstances ever bring you into Minnesota, I hope you'll feel free to give me a call. I'm still in the public relations field, now working for a consulting firm in downtown St. Paul. It would be a great pleasure to see you again, and to compare notes on where our lives have taken us since we last met.

A very Good wish for your continued success . . .

Sincerely,

Marsha K.
St. Paul, Minn.

The "serious illness" that Marsha referred to was the key to the control that the Assemblies of God managed to exert over me. In that desperate situation, I allowed myself to become dependent upon those "knowledgeable" Christian leaders. What's worse, I led others down that same path.

My "testimony" of being miraculously healed of cancer became the pivotal point of the message I preached during the ten years I was an evangelist. The Assemblies of God greatly encouraged this, and I sincerely believed it to be true.

It all started in the early 1970s, soon after I had publicly become a born-again Christian. It made little sense to me that I would be stricken in this fashion, right after dedicating my life to God. Yes, I had a panic attack when the bleeding started and the doctor gave me his diagnosis. I shared this somber news with my new Christian brothers.

"Of course, this doesn't make any sense," one said. "Can't you see that this is the devil trying to discourage you from serving God." It fascinated me that his statement, framed as a question, was spoken as a declaration. The declarative-question could effectively become the final word. I bought it.

Collectively, the brothers and sisters of the Assemblies of God convinced me that God would heal me. God had allowed this to happen in order to show His healing power. Following their advice,

I attended a Full Gospel Business Men's Fellowship International (FGBMFI) meeting held at the Hotel New Yorker in Manhattan. All of the pentecostals I knew, including my daughter's piano teacher, declared that when I came home from that meeting I would be totally healed. With such an elaborate support system, I found myself primed and ready to receive healing. After the evangelist Robert Thom prayed for me, I agreed with him in front of the audience that God had healed me. Praise the Lord!

Following the prayer I was told to "hold on" to my healing. If any of the old symptoms connected with the cancer should "crop up," I should reject those "false" symptoms as a "temptation of Satan to get me to turn loose of my healing."

Another minister at the meeting, pointing to Kenneth Hagin's teachings, explained it this way:

> Hebrews 11:1 says, "Now faith is the substance of things hoped for, the evidence of things not seen." The EVIDENCE of your healing is the fact that you claimed it in the name of Jesus Christ, and your FAITH will stand in the place of your total healing until Satan turns loose of the symptoms and he will because he MUST.

This is standard Assemblies of God teaching.

Completely assured, I discontinued medical advice and rejoiced over the miracle, which I accepted with no further questions.

The Assemblies of God published a miniature booklet entitled "The Ringmaster Meets Jesus," which announced to the world my victory over cancer through God's intervention. Preachers throughout the denomination heralded it as a great example of God's healing power. All Assemblies of God churches opened up to me and I was invited to testify about my personal miracle. The more I preached it, the more I believed it. I became increasingly generous with my money out of gratitude to the Assemblies of God. This sensational testimony, coming from a circus ringmaster, assured big crowds and big offerings for the churches I visited. Many people followed my example of relying totally upon God for their healing instead of receiving the medical treatment they really needed.

While relying upon what the Assemblies of God leaders were pumping into me, I found myself undergoing a private struggle. My energy level seemed to be decreasing. I had little stamina. Something pressing on the inside of me caused me considerable discomfort. Giving my circus performances became difficult. I knew (having been forewarned) that the devil had me under siege. I needed to hold onto my faith. After all, that's what the Bible said.

In 1976, after being persuaded to leave show business to devote myself full-time to the ministry ("You can't keep one foot in the world and expect to be a true Christian"), I faced a real test. Almost immediately, a severe "false symptom" erupted. To my shock I began urinating dark heavy blood. This happened in Pittsburgh while I was preparing to speak to the Charismatic Conference, ironically, about my cancer healing.

My Christian brothers and sisters reassured me. "Isn't this just so obvious? The Devil would like nothing better than to keep you from giving your testimony before 10,000 people here. Probably a lot of people would be healed after hearing your testimony. Can't you see that the Devil has thrown on you false symptoms of your cancer to scare you and keep you from serving God?"

I had heard so many dedicated Christians saying the same words that I accepted what they told me. I went out to the platform and fulfilled my speaking engagement. After my talk and prayer offering for the sick, many people stood and claimed to have been miraculously healed. It appeared that the Christians were absolutely right in what they had been telling me. I could not lean on my own understanding. I ignored the critical warning to seek medical help and continued as a minister and evangelist for the next ten years.

In 1982, the slow deterioration of my health suggested that maybe I had not been healed after all. I had fallen out of favor with the Assemblies of God. After that sect had managed to bilk me out of the last of my savings, they closed their churches to me. They wanted nothing more to do with me. To justify their actions, they spread horrible lies about me throughout North America.

In April 1989, when *Don't Call Me Brother* was ready for publication, I finally sought medical advice. The doctor found the tumor and wanted to hospitalize me immediately. I had accepted a three-month tour with The Reid Brothers Circus beginning that same month and did not want to cancel it. I desperately needed the income. The Assemblies of God had left me flat broke and in debt.

I felt that an additional three-month delay of what I had begun to think of as the inevitable would be of little consequence. The more than eighteen-year time lapse since the cancer had been first discovered was too great a time to even hope that the deadly disease had not spread.

Following the circus tour, a biopsy confirmed the active cancer in my body. Only my immediate family knew of this. We kept this intense private battle a secret from the public. I wrapped up several radio and TV interviews, including "The Sally Jessy Raphael Show," made a quick trip to Los Angeles to do "The Tom Leykis Show" on KFI Radio and "The John Stewart Show" on KKLA, then drove back home, arriving in the wee hours. The next morning I checked into a hospital.

Early that Monday morning, September 11, 1989, I faced the radical surgery that would determine my future. The five-hour operation, performed by three doctors, was 100% successful. They got it all. Incredibly, the cancer had not spread, despite overwhelming odds. After two days in intensive care, my rapid and complete recovery astonished everyone.

I returned home that same week, on September 17. The next day I began a full schedule of telephone radio interviews from my home. The only thing that slowed me down was the catheter they had hooked me up to. I hated that thing. My poodle, however, thought it was the greatest thing he had ever seen. Why, he has to pee on a bush to establish territory, but to be able to carry it around in a plastic bag for the world to see . . . now that is real power!

One night I yelled out from my bedroom, "I want to get rid of this thing!" That was all that Deputy, my poodle, needed to hear. Just as I dozed off, he trotted into the room, picked up that bag in his mouth, and with me still attached started to run off with it. Shirley Ann caught him just in time.

I finally got rid of that instrument of torture on September 27. The next day, exactly two and a half weeks after the surgery, I made my first public appearances. I did a studio radio interview with Barry Martin on KVON in the California wine country and then spoke at the Napa Kiwanis Club. By the third week of October I once again began hopping airplanes for TV interviews around the country.

With the cancer out of my body, I have the highest energy level I've ever known. Best of all, there were no side effects from the surgery. I was damn lucky. Not everyone who believed the church for a "faith healing" has been so fortunate. I cannot help but wonder how many lives I may have hurt with my "testimony" that encouraged people to "look to God for their healing." This thought constantly haunts me. To those people who may have been hurt as a result, I ask forgiveness. I really believed that God had performed a miracle of healing in my life. Then again . . . considering the extraordinary circumstances . . . maybe He did.

IV

A Way with Words

The Lord gave the word: great was the company of those that published it.

Psalms 68:11

Raymond, Ill.
June 14, 1989

Dear Mr. Miles:

I just finished reading your book and want you to know I believe your story. Although, I do not feel you care what anyone thinks at this point.

Nevertheless, if you had not leaned on the arm of flesh and had fallen in love with the Lord Jesus Christ and had taken the time to know and love the greatest life on earth, maybe you would not feel as you do today. People will fail you, but never the Lord.

I can understand how you must feel after all that has happened to you, but I feel a root of bitterness has sprung up in your heart and it will eventually destroy you. I have had abuses by other church people and always wondered how they could do such things and love the Lord, but my faith remains strong because of my Lord.

I also feel you are being hypocritical, when on the one hand you were railroaded by rumors and then on page 302 you said, "it was reported Swaggart was back cruising the same seedy motel strip in New Orleans." Sounds like rumors to me and I'm not upholding Swaggart at all. He sinned and should step down.

Throughout your book, you mentioned "this fed my ego," etc. Maybe that was your problem, too much ego. I feel too many television ministers love the limelight. There are no stars in this walk. Stars fall. Regardless, God is the same every day, He doesn't change, only people and God has the final judgment of all people and each person will be judged individually for their deeds, but it will be much harder for those who once knew and slipped back.

Mr. Cohen's assessment of the church is not true at all. Both of you are putting all Christians in one lump. God knows who are His. I have a real born-again experience and I don't have to put it in quotes, I know. You are poking fun at God and all His followers who know they have eternal life. Remember God is not mocked. In 1 John 2:19, "They went out from us, but they were not of us." You can be the judge of this. If I had known you were not following Christ any longer I would not have bought your book. All it is doing is making you richer. The rich young ruler would not follow Christ because he trusted in his riches. When we come to the end of our way, nothing will matter but what we have done with Christ.

May God help you along this journey called life. Corruption and sin is rampant in America and it won't be long, it will all be over. Whatever you yield yourself to obey, that will be your master. Romans 6:16.

Sincerely,

Mrs. John R. Gudgel

I wrote back to Mrs. Gudgel. Along with asking permission to print her letter, I asked her also to please reread *Don't Call Me Brother*. No one who truthfully reads that book can come to the conclusion that I mocked God. To Mrs. Gudgel and the multitude of like-minded Christians who fear that my book will "only make me richer," please don't lose sleep over this concern. It would be impossible for me to make a single dime in profit on *Don't Call Me Brother*. My research cost me too much.

Mrs. Gudgel's response turned out to be a pleasant surprise.

December 19, 1989

Dear Mr. Miles:

In view of all that has happened in the Church of Jesus Christ, we could stand a positive perspective of what a Christian really is.

Please accept my apology for judging the hurt you experienced. As long as we are on this earth, I guess there will be gross human error. We strive for perfection, but with some it is hard to attain, and I'm talking mainly about myself.

I see no problem in using the letter in your new book.

May God richly bless you in all your endeavors. Merry Christmas and Happy New Year.

Sincerely,

Mrs. John R. Gudgel

P.S. I hope you bring us up to date with what has transpired since the last book.

Many Christians who criticized my book and motives have apologized since Jim Bakker's trial and conviction. The truth in what I have brought forth can no longer be ignored or denied.

Others, unfortunately, continue to cling to their belief system with rigid tenacity and to unflinchingly protect those who preach it. Doing so serves to enforce a kind of projected righteousness in their own lives. This displays to the world what godly people they are, despite what lurks beneath the surface or whom they hurt in the process. If God's in it, it's gotta be good!

This response did not come by letter, but in the pages of *Circus Report*, a show business trade paper, published in the October 9, 1989, issue. This one came as a jolt. First of all, because it came from a member of my beloved circus profession; second, because it was from a performer I knew and believed was a friend. I should have learned by now to never be surprised by anything spawned by a Christian.

IN THE MAIL

from Sharon Ward

Austin Miles, self-styled "Reverend," ringmaster, author, is now doing another turn, as authority on corruption in the Christian ministry. His book, *Don't Call Me Brother*, blasting televangelists for exploiting God for personal gain is selling for $20 a copy.

Along with radio programs, TV appearances and magazine interviews it is apparent that he has learned from his theatrical background and the Bakkers about achieving fame by association for fun and profit.

Of course there are people calling themselves Christians who betray our trust, but we don't abandon our relationship with God because of it anymore than we would stop reading books because of disreputable authors.

The judgment of Jim and Tammy Bakker will be the same whether or not other people use their misfortunes to earn a living.

Last year Austin was again in the limelight in CR [*Circus Report*] because of alleged CIA harassment. Having been on the receiving end perhaps a little compassion would be in order here.

The Bible tells us that "all have sinned" so who, then, can cast the first stone . . . even for profit? (Matt. 18:6–7)

Will the real Alvie Maddox* please stand up.

Circus Report published my reply on October 23, 1989:

AUSTIN RESPONDS

Sharon Ward's criticism of me and my book (CR 10/9/89) was a cheap shot, in an apparent attempt to gain recognition for her own pious lifestyle at my expense. As is so often

---

*Alvie Maddox was Austin Miles's previous name.

the case with born-again Christians, she obviously had not read the book that she finds so offensive.

Don't Call Me Brother has made the "Best Selling Religious Book" list. It is in its sixth printing with a seventh printing being scheduled. The heavy volume of responses I am receiving is so fascinating that I am doing another book titled *Setting the Captives Free*. This work will be out in the autumn of 1990.

Ninty-eight percent of the responses to my book have been positive. Surprisingly, the majority of Christians who have read my book and responded have thanked me for writing it, including members and former members of the Assemblies of God and a limited number of A.G. ministers. Several mainline ministers have held the book up from their pulpits and advised their people to read it. Miss Ward's public denouncement of me and my book will gain for her the recognition she craves, ". . . pressed down, and shaken together, and running over . . ." (St. Luke 6:38). I will print her article in my new book along with a brief analysis of the life behind her judgmental attitude.

Miss Ward's article made me angry enough to want to publish some jagged facts about her lifestyle. But then, in assessing that possibility, I realized that at the time Miss Ward shared her personal story so openly with me it had not been made absolutely clear that I no longer had any involvement in the ministry. Therefore, I must consider what she told me about herself confidential. Even though I am not in the ministry now, and have no plans ever to be again, I respect the position I once held and would never violate any trust that came through it.

The circus world has changed drastically since Christianity managed to get its icy grip on this once tightly knit, family-oriented, loyal group. Regrettably, my influence helped to encourage this, when my zeal as a born-again Christian could not be contained. The public attack on me by a fellow performer is a consequence of that.

Before Christianity came to the circus, divorce and adultery were virtually unheard of. I never saw stealing, cheating, alcoholism, drug abuse, or juvenile delinquency. Family members worked together, traveled together, played together, and genuinely liked one another. Thanks to Christianity, dividing lines have been drawn up in the circus between born-agains and non-born-agains—sometimes within the same family. The wonderful camraderie that once prevailed backstage is no more. Sexual morality has loosened up, divorce has become rampant, drugs and alcohol have come in.

Enroute to a circus date, the stepmother of a very famous family wound up stranded on the side of the highway due to a mechanical breakdown of her truck. She knew the rest of the circus was behind her. Her stepson and his wife, both devout born-agains, sped down the highway, saw her stranded on the side, and passed her by, making no effort to stop and help her. They didn't want to be late for a prayer meeting.

A *non*-born-again circus couple saw her, stopped, and helped her on her way. When the woman arrived in the next town, she found her stepson and his wife with the other circus born-agains, sitting in a circle by their trailers, with open Bibles in their laps. She walked over to her stepson and with a powerful upswing knocked the Bible out of his hand. "This is bullshit!" she blasted. "You're supposed to be such a great Christian, and you leave your mother stranded on the side of the road so you can get to a prayer meeting." She shot a glance at the rest of them. "You're *all* full of shit!"

The old stereotype of criminals in the circus became a reality *after* Christianity came in. A hardened, vicious criminal who had been put in prison for armed robbery and assault, a brute of a man, became gloriously "saved" while in prison. A born-again circus woman met him, married him, and he became part of the show with a small elephant act. He fancied himself as a minister and had biblical quotes all over his truck.

Taking great offense at me when a news story came out about the book I was writing, he cornered me backstage just before a show in Poughkeepsie, New York, with an elephant hook in his hand and threatened me with physical harm. The police were called and bodyguards were assigned to me for the remainder of that engagement.

The circus that I loved so much is no more. Alas, the Christians convinced us that they had what we needed.

V

Coming as an Angel of Light

Hear this, all ye people; give ear, all ye inhabitants of the world:
Both low and high, rich and poor, together.

                                                        Psalms 49:1-2

I have received several letters that could not be included here—
the writers are fighting in the courts to reclaim families who have
been mentally kidnaped by the Assemblies of God church. To publish
their letters could possibly complicate the proceedings. I had just
completed the chapter about the division of circus families due to
Christianity when four such letters arrived in the mail. Each of the
four cases of family disruption started with the children being
approached and recruited in public schools.

Once the children were coaxed into the "born-again spirit-filled"
experience, they were taught that anyone, *including their own parents*,
who had not gone through this ritual was an enemy of the faith.
One bewildered older couple, who faithfully attended a mainline
church, told me they were suddenly rejected by their grandchildren.
How could a once-loving family be torn apart so quickly?

Two separate letters came from heartbroken husbands whose
wives had filed divorce papers against them. Their children had been
recruited in school, and the wives joined their children in the
Assemblies of God pentecostal belief system. The husbands objected,
and divorce proceedings resulted.

Horrible rumors and false accusations were leveled against
victims who tried to prevent a family member from joining that
cult. A lawyer representing one family whose children were damaged

by the Assemblies of God church wrote me to ask if I knew any deprogrammers. "It is my impression," he wrote, "that the children will require this deprogramming procedure in order to regain any semblance of normalcy."

In another instance of remarkable timing, these letters arrived on the very same day an Associated Press story confirmed that the Assemblies of God wants to recruit students openly in the high schools, by way of "Bible Clubs." To the unsuspecting, this might sound harmless. Mrs. Bridget Mergens Mayhew, a Nebraska housewife, mother, and staunch adherent of the Assembly of God in Omaha, had traveled to Washington, D.C., to present her petition to the Supreme Court. As a result, on June 4, 1990, by an 8-1 vote, the high court ruled that Westside High School in Omaha must allow a Christian "Bible Club" to be organized on its campus.

On the day following the historic ruling, a gloating Pat Robertson declared to his "700 Club" viewers: "This is wonderful! This represents a great victory for evangelicals. This ruling means that students are now free to carry their Bibles openly and read them in the public schools *and hand out tracts!*" Robertson went on to state that his own Christian Coalition, with lawyers funded by viewer's contributions to the tax-exempt "700 Club," would be present in every city and town to make sure the mandate of the court is carried out, so that Christians will be able to operate on high-school campuses without hindrance.

First of all, make no mistake about it, the Assemblies of God is a *cult.* Their motivation is total control and power over people. The best way to accomplish this is to start with the young, our kids. This is achieved by steady indoctrination and by separating novices from anyone and everyone who asks questions or objects to their involvement, especially family members and good friends. Countless families and friendships have been torn apart in the church's fierce battle for disciples.

The Christian leaders have the words of Jesus to back them up. Check out these surprising verses in St. Matthew 10: 34-37:

34. Think not that I am come to send peace on earth: I came not to send peace, but a sword.

35. For I am come to set a man at variance against his father, and the daughter against her mother, and the daughter in law against her mother in law.

36. And a man's foes shall be they of his own household.
[Author's note: According to Assemblies of God teaching,
this Scripture means that the greatest enemy of your faith
is your own family.]

37. He that loveth father or mother more than me is
not worthy of me: and he that loveth son or daughter more
than me is not worthy of me.

Shocking? You bet it is. Now, let's take it one step farther with
St. Luke 14: 26—again the words of Jesus that the church preaches:

If any man come to me, *and hate not his father and mother, and
wife, and children,* and brethren, and sisters, yea, and his own
life also, *he cannot be my disciple.* [Emphasis added]

We should all closely examine the Bible, and the words found therein,
which the Assemblies of God want to contaminate our children
with—in the public schools yet, out of our sight. It is also time
to seriously question the Bible and its authenticity. Are these really
the words of God, or the Son of God? I think not.

Once a family member or friend is sucked into such a cult it
is extremely difficult to get him or her out. I am still estranged
from my daughter, Lori. According to an acquaintance in Millville,
New Jersey, who saw Lori with her new baby in a store in 1988,
I have a grandson, whom I have never seen. My grandson had
obviously been born only a couple of weeks before. That is all the
information I have. In what can only be described as satanic, the
Assemblies of God Church takes great pleasure in the heartache
it has caused me, sharing this news gleefully with anyone who will
listen.

Charles Roman diverted his calling as a young evangelist to
enter medical school after witnessing such vicious deeds by his
denomination. He told me of a conversation he had with Rev. Jerry
L. Sturgeon, pastor of the Mainland Assembly of God Church in
Linwood, New Jersey. I have never met or spoken to Rev. Sturgeon.
When my name came up, a look of sadistic delight spread across
his face as he said, "Have you heard? Austin Miles's daughter doesn't
even speak to him." He seems to be saying: "Isn't it wonderful what
we've been able to accomplish in the name of Jesus?"

We can no longer sit by idly and *allow* the church to continue such abuses. Here is what we can, and *must* do. Those of us who have been hurt by the church should not suffer silently. This is exactly what the church wants. We should make our experience public in every way we can. Those who have a flair for writing should write newspaper articles, letters to the editor, magazine pieces, even a book. I have proved that this can be done and have an effect. But we need more such stories in print. Send your letters to me— I will continue to publish them. Make your voices heard for the sake of future victims. If enough people tell the truth about the church, maybe those whose minds are still shackled will begin to realize that they are being held captive by a lie, and find the strength and the resolve to finally break free.

If enough people would stand up and be counted, there could be enough pressure to demand that the legislators pass some protective laws. Begin filing lawsuits against alienation of family members by the church, wrongful death in faith healing cases, incompetent counseling by pastors. Make police reports *immediately* when your child is molested by a preacher or priest, and *let no one dissuade you.* When a pastor sexually violates you, report it. Minnesota is the first state to pass a law that requires a prison sentence for any minister that has sexual relations with a parishioner. I would like to see every state in America follow suit. Lawyers are now aware of a new age of the church tort and are open to pursue such cases. Above all, no matter how sweet these people seem to be, don't hesitate to possibly offend them by refusing to accept what they're selling. Your family is more important than offending these misfits. Protect your family.

It cannot be too strongly emphasized that in this new but troublesome age the family *unit* must be restructured and defined. Family *unity* must be the first and foremost priority of every home. This may take sacrifice and self discipline, such as turning off the television set to listen to one another, or cutting down on the booze so there is more energy for each other. A protective shield should be put around every member of your household.

The home should be a protected sanctuary where only kind, encouraging words are spoken, and love without fear can be expressed. No intrusion should be allowed by any person who could bring a restless and possibly unhealthy spirit inside.

The next letter shows why such precautions are a necessity. Even though this is not a church situation, the methods of mind control and manipulation used on this victim are the same. The city has been disguised and the names have been changed. But the names will have a special meaning to the victim we are trying to reach, and will hopefully bring her back to her family.

Pittsburgh, Pa.
September 27, 1989

Dear Mr. Miles:

I am the person who called you after hearing your discussion on radio today concerning your experiences and your book, *Don't Call Me Brother.* Thank you so much for being kind enough to listen. The longer this goes on, the less people want to hear about it. People tend to blame her, when I know the problem began with and resulted from this young man's evil manipulation. Relatives, close friends, and everyone who knows our family and our daughter cannot believe any of this. Every morning I awake thinking it must be a nightmare. It could not be how 17½ years of a loving daughter in a loving family could end.

I was touched by your final statement this morning about not allowing anyone to brainwash someone you love and take that person from you. The pain you have endured in the loss of your wife and your daughter is the pain we are feeling in the loss of our daughter. You know that what you were led to do was not what you would have done without outside pressure, influence, and mind control. We know this is the case with our daughter.

Allison was a beautiful, 17-year-old honor student in her senior year of high school. She was active in school, popular, a volunteer for the elderly and handicapped, a leader, a band officer. She had always shown excellent taste in friends and dates. There were no problems at all—no drugs, no alcohol. She dropped her friends who began drinking. She was the most kind, compassionate, and caring of our four children.

From the very moment she met this person, he has lied, conned, and brainwashed our daughter against us. He is definitely a "cult" of one. He lied about having had a drunk-driving conviction. He lied about previous marriages. He would chide her about calling home when she was out or about meeting her curfews (both of which she always did pleasantly). He pulled her away more and more, and talked her into disregarding rules and showing little respect.

He followed her to college last fall. We were shocked when she came home in early spring, having asked a college classmate to help her escape from him. She told her friend that he had beaten her, that she and her mom were best friends until this guy turned her against me, etc. She told us she was sorry and that she regretted everything she had done since meeting him.

We were so relieved that she had found out what he really was. She promised she would have nothing more to do with him—that she was too valuable, that she wasn't stupid, that she hated all that had happened. That whole week she was her old self—she had three dates lined up, she was seeing old friends, we went to lunch, shopping, had our hair done. She was looking forward to the future.

At the end of the week, this guy contacted her. We begged her not to see him—we were afraid he would hurt her. She said she could handle it and wouldn't do anything stupid.

When she returned from seeing him that night, she was in his web again. She even had a different look about her, a different edge to her voice. She told us she still cared for him. We told her we felt he was dangerous; and, after all she had told us, we could no longer support any relationship with him.

I was to take her back to college the next morning. During the night he had come and talked her into leaving with him by her bedroom window. A friend of hers says he threatened suicide if she didn't return with him.

He got her an answering machine, so we can't make any contact with her by telephone. We don't know if she gets our mail—he's destroyed other people's mail.

Since she left, we've had this guy investigated by every person and organization you can imagine. We found out that he was a wife abuser. A public beating at a restaurant is on file. He has lied to her about high school, his position in the army, his army discharge (a less than honorable discharge for violence). He is a suspect in a very serious crime and may currently be involved in criminal activity. He isn't paying his bills. We are afraid of what will happen if he leaves her or gets arrested. He's forced her to alienate herself from family and friends. She's cut off her support group. She may feel she has no place to go. That is not true because we love her and would welcome her back with open arms at any point.

We know she's been brainwashed, because she doesn't even stay in contact with a relative she loved who is in a home and really doesn't even know anything about the situation. The Allison we knew would never hurt anyone. She was spotted in town several times but never called. She has no contact with her brothers and sister at college or at home. We left a box of birthday gifts for her at his family's home—we never even got a thank you. This is absolutely not her—she was always buying cards and remembering important days in people's lives. She hasn't placed a phone call here in six months. We don't even know whether she's alive from one week to the next.

If he were not dangerous and she were not brainwashed, conned and lied to, we could sit back and know time would take care of everything—that she will find out for herself. But she could be seriously hurt by that time. As it stands now, if she ever comes out of this, she will need much treatment to deal with her emotional and mental state.

She has allowed this person to back her into a corner, isolate her from her support group, keep her from learning the truth about this person.

I've asked her by letter to please meet with me, just so we can hug and say we love each other (we were very close). I told her one relationship doesn't mean you can't have another. She doesn't even answer.

Authorities spout legalities at us—she's 18, and it's her right to like someone bad. But everyone knows this is so totally out of character for Allison, and she doesn't even know what he is or what he has done. He has more rights as a criminal type than we do as parents, or she has to know that she could be living with a very dangerous person. Even if she were told, would she not believe and further jeopardize her life by carrying this information back to him?

We are broken-hearted, we are worried sick for her safety, we don't sleep because she doesn't know what we know and has turned against us on the basis of his lies and brainwashing. Even his stepsister told me he is very manipulative and that she wouldn't want him with her daughter.

I know there are no easy answers—maybe there are no answers at all. My purpose in contacting you was to ask from your experience, what made you realize you were being used, do you have any ideas of where to turn that we may not have thought of, is there anything we are missing in our attempt to rescue her from his grasp? Some people say to forget her—we could never do that. We love her so much, and we fear for her life. We can never stop trying.

I'm about to go out and get your book. Maybe I can learn something from it. I feel so bad that you have lost what you have. You are in our prayers. You are quite right that the two things we can do are pray and let her know we love her. Thank you for your prayers. We hope life will be better to you. God bless you.

Sincerely,

Amy and Jay MacMillan

As the next letter shows, no matter what label is given to the church of Jesus Christ, the purpose seems to be the same in all of them: divide and conquer the family for the sake of the Gospel.

Kitchener, Ontario, Canada
November 12, 1989

Dear Brother Austin,

I feel I can call you that because after reading your book *Don't Call Me Brother* I'm part of the "family."

I was a Jehovah's Witness for 21½ years—And though I never witnessed the sexual discrepancies you did, I've suffered the gossip & shunning you have. I was disfellowshipped after serving the Watchtower for all those years.

I truly believed it was God's organization. My husband used to beg me to stop studying with these people—But *I* believed he was a "tool of Satan." The reason I was disfellowshipped? Because I *could not preach* 1914 Armageddon. I can sympathize with you. But maybe Rose Marie will read the book. My husband is dead, so he'll never know how sorry I was, & am. I was "chucked out" a year after he died.

My daughter and grandchildren are told not to talk to me. They are still in "Bondage."

I'm so afraid to trust *any* religion now. I believe in the Lord Jesus Christ but I'm too tired at 62 yrs. to study & learn. All I know is *"He* died for me" & I don't care where I go.

If *He* wants to use me I've told Him, I'm willing, But how, when & where, is *His* decision. As long as *He* gives me the strength, wisdom, *Not* Man.

Sincerely, I remain,
Grace Gough

P.S. I'm thinking of writing a book entitled *You Used To Call Me Sister.*

Grace G. says that she is "afraid to trust any religion." She does not have to, and is certainly better off not to.

The church gains power by plunging people down into a murky pit of self-worthlessness. By stripping away self-esteem from the believer and forever keeping him in the throes of dreadful guilt, which needs constant forgiveness, the church exerts absolute control over its followers. It is all done subtly and skillfully. Most of the sheep don't even realize they've been shorn.

This is why, even after a severe burning and an earnest attempt to leave the church, the devotee will still try to hang onto religion, any religion. Church brainwashing is difficult to counteract. It takes real strength, and sometimes outside help, to break way.

Here is a Mormon point of view on the guilt-and-fear tactic.

Western U.S.
September 11, 1989

Dear Mr. Miles,

I just finished reading *Don't Call Me Brother*, and I'm writing to thank you for writing it. A friend of mine is a talk show host at a local radio station. She loaned the book to me, probably thinking I would appreciate your story because of my own life's experience. Perhaps you recall her interview with you. I did not hear the interview myself.

I noticed in the picture section that it is soon your 56th birthday, so Happy Birthday! I hope your life has become more peaceful and satisfying by now, although the PTL trials are still getting tremendous press. If there is a Divine hand in this mess, He seems to have gotten you out just in time.

Your willingness to share your intimate thoughts and feelings made the book very human and real. You obviously still care deeply about other people. I was touched by how objective you were able to remain, given the depth of sacrifice and sorrow & disappointment you endured.

I certainly was taken aback by your revelations of the powers and unbridled freedoms of the F.B.I. That part frightened me the most. I hope the "force" has taken you off their harassment list. So much for the notion of "with liberty & justice for all."

I was rather bemused by the fact that in the conviction of the Taggart Brothers yesterday, no mention was made of Bakker's homosexual relationship with David Taggart. I wonder how they managed to exclude that piece of trivia from the story. What a zoo!

I think I'll read Cohen's book *The Mind of the Bible Believer* next. Thanks for introducing it in your book. I think it would be helpful to me, in part, in understanding the mind of a Mormon. I was raised as a fundamental Mormon, but I can no longer ignore what I know goes on in the big business of the church. Mormons have their own version of self-righteous, judgmental, arrogant blindness. I wonder if I could become objective enough, and find a place for all my disappointment, that I could write a book about my experiences as the wife of a controller of one of the financial areas of the Mormon Church—a similarly disillusioning experience to yours.

Someone once said to me, "I could never work for the church. . . . I prefer my fantasies about it." With good reason. Most Mormons I know feel that way, I think.

I support you in enduring the inevitable backlash of "righteous indignation" from the "Christian" Community. Your book helped me, and I believe will help any honest person who has not lost all dignity & self-respect to the "forgiveness brokers" of big business Christianity.

The Christian religions, including Mormonism, cannot reconcile the conflict between the doctrine of "choosing goodness" and "non judgment." Just saying the word "good" presences [sic] judgment. They cannot keep one doctrine without violating the other. That leaves them permanently in sin, permanently needing forgiveness & permanently ready to sacrifice money, family and health for it.

I agree with your opinion regarding the tax-exempt status of churches. Why should hard-working, decent minded people have to shoulder the extra burden of taxes which churches don't have to pay, in order for those churches to continue this emotional blackmail they call "giving oneself to the Lord"?

Well, I can see this letter is getting long. You can tell I was affected by your writing. Thank you, and good luck to you.

Sincerely,
Linda H.

L. H. has gone through the experience and exhibits a natural talent for writing. I encourage her to write that book. It is needed.

Baker, Oreg.
September 3, 1989

Dear Austin:

Thanks for having the guts to write *Don't Call Me Brother*. Just as surely as the sun rises and sets, everything in life has a reason. Hopefully this book will set many goody-goody Christians on the right road to enlightenment. Organized religion is a money-making scheme. By creating guilt and fear of the unknown it keeps the flock in bondage.

Read Joseph Campbell's books, one of which is the *Power of Myth* with Bill Moyers. His books will take you around the world viewing the history of religious myths illustrating the power over the ignorant. Christianity is nothing but a copy.

Search the old bookstores for a copy of *The World's Sixteen Crucified Saviors* by Lydia M. Graves, copyright 1875. The title tells the story, well documented book, that should convince you once and for all that organized Christian religions are copies created for a purpose.

Bertrand Russell maintains that what men need is not dogma, but rather an attitude of Christian love of compassion. "Christians hold that their faith does good, but other faiths do harm. At any rate, they hold this about the Communist faith. What I wish to maintain is that all faiths do harm. We may define faith as a firm belief in something for which there is no evidence. When there is evidence, no one speaks of faith. We do not speak of faith that two and two are four or that the earth is round. We only speak of faith when we wish to substitute emotion for evidence." I believe Shirley MacLaine is on the right track. Her first books well illustrate her stumbling and seeking for something higher. Her latest book *Going Within* is a guide for inner transformation. Man's destiny is an individual matter between himself and God, not a matter for the authority of the Church to decide. No one author has all the truth. I believe the truth is quite simple, consciousness is the key. Consciousness is the cause as well as the substance of the entire world.

Search the world and reclaim your dear Rose Marie. It is loud and clear to me that she is your soul mate. And don't go back and dwell on regrets. Find Rose Marie and tell her you love her. I love her too. And, I hope you make a million on your book. You deserve it, and more.

With Love,

Vivian H.

It is interesting to note that not one born-again Pentecostal expressed concern over my devastating divorce from Rose Marie. On the contrary, these church-going Christians were delighted to see the destruction of my family. The people who have reached out to me in great warmth and friendship have been the un-churched.

For several years I did everything possible to reclaim Rose Marie and my marriage. That desperate, heartbreaking time contributed to the eventual breakdown of my health.

If anything would have brought us back together, it would have been that extraordinary one-in-ten-million chance meeting in Macy's Santaland. By that time it was too late. I have heard nothing from her since. Former acquaintances from that period of my life tell me that she has not remarried. I do not know if she has seen or read my book. That part of my personal story, which is told in *Don't Call Me Brother*, ended there. Not for the born-agains, however. They are still happily taking their bows for what they were able to accomplish. In their demented way of thinking, this represents power.

Tacoma, Wash.
November 17, 1989

Mr. Austin Miles:

I heard you on a radio program and made a note of it and tried to find your excellent book at the local bookstores. I was able to get a copy at the library and enjoyed reading it so much that I then tried again to locate a copy for my daughter as a Christmas present, and to read it again.

I finally had to order one and I asked the bookseller why they didn't order an extra for the shelf so that others could read it, and how could it get on the best seller list if it was not available.

Their answer, "That they had nothing to do with the best sellers, that that was determined all across the country."

How do we get this excellent book on the shelves?

I could have easily been caught up in this movement if my wife hadn't objected so strenuously.

A great beautiful church here burned to the ground, and I'll always believe that it was torched by a disgruntled husband whose wife was completely taken in by the cult. I knew one man that was of that mentality, and was actually sick because of his wife's involvement.

A great book Mr. Miles. That and some of Mark Twain's writings that I have recently read, has changed my thinking considerably.

Respectfully,

Earl Keehn

I received another letter from Mr. Keehn.

Tacoma, Wash.
December 8, 1989

Dear Mr. Miles:

This little article appeared this morning in our newspaper. [A man had successfully sued the FBI for unlawful interference and harassment.] I immediately thought of you and am wondering if now you could take action against the FBI.

I just finished reading your excellent book again and our Christmas letters will all be promoting your book. I hope that you make back your lost fortune with your writings.

Years ago when I got involved with the church it caused so much trouble in the family that in desperation I went to the preacher for counseling. He quoted the Scripture, "Be ye not unequally yoked together," suggesting that perhaps we should separate if she would not join with me in my beliefs.

After wrestling with it for a few days I decided that the here and now was more important than a nebulous future in the hereafter.

Your book gave me so much comfort, and reinforced my thinking that I had made the right decision.

My best wishes to you for this season and for all the rest of your life. Would love to meet you sometime. If you are ever in this area, there is room in our house and transportation.

Till When,

Earl Keehn

The Scripture verse that Mr. Keehn referred to is 2 Corinthians 6:14:

Be ye not unequally yoked together with unbelievers: for what fellowship hath righteousness with unrighteousness? and what communion hath light with darkness?

Countless victims whose marriages have been destroyed by the church have told me that this is the Scripture verse that a pastor cited to convince their spouse to break up their marriage. During radio interviews in various parts of the United States I have received several on-air telephone calls from the hapless survivors of such sabotaged marriages. They all tell me the same story: 2 Corinthians 6:14. Perhaps the Bible should be subtitled: "Words to Break Up a Family By."

June 8, 1989

Mr. Miles,

I called in to KFYI in Phoenix when you were on the air yesterday. I mentioned a support group here called Second Chance, which is for ex-cult members. You wanted some information on our group so I have included a newspaper article.

We meet once per month, and there are usually about 4–8 people at the meetings. We basically discuss any problems we are having readjusting to "normal" society, show videotapes like "Marjoe," and plan ways to provide information to the public. We have been in existence since January of this year.

You may be interested to know that there is a national group called FOCUS, affiliated with the Cult Awareness

Network, which is a loose-knit organization of ex-cult members. Local chapters of FOCUS often have support groups such as ours. You can get more information from:

CAN (Cult Awareness Network)
2421 W. Pratt Blvd., Suite 1173
Chicago, Illinois 60645
(312) 267-7777

I had been in the United Pentecostal Church for six years, and you may be interested to know that besides my own pastor there were several pastors who were transferred rather than expelled even when the national office knew how bad these people were. My opinion of this is that the national office fears that many pastors would leave their organization to become independent churches, thus weakening the national office.

Thank you for a good program, and I look forward to reading your book. If you need any information from me, please feel free to contact me.

Sincerely,

Jeff Jacobsen
Phoenix, Ariz.

Grand Rapids, Mich.
November 22, 1989

Dear Mr. Miles:

How I ached as I read your book! Not that it wasn't fascinating reading, because it was. Extremely so. But I, too, was hurt, damaged so much by the church that when I hear of someone injured so brutally it just hurts me to the quick.

I wasn't reared in pentacostalism but I wasn't too much removed from that approach. I was a holiness child, which means that I was raised in much the same style except for the "tongues." The holiness branch of Methodism ignored tongues and the rest of the "gifts" except I do remember "anointing" services when individuals were anointed with oil for healing.

Whereas you stumbled into pentacostalism as an adult, I was conceived in the womb of holiness and nursed at the bosom of all the legalism, anger, hypocrisy, guilt, frustration that I was surrounded with during my formative years.

To share it all with you, I'd have to write my own book, and I won't be able to condense it all here. Let me just briefly say that when I was sixteen I was told by my pastor when I admitted to having jealousy and envy that "I'd never get to heaven if I had jealousy in my life." As an afterthought he added that that statement wasn't his own, it was what the Bible stated. Alas! The trouble was that I believed him. What I was afraid of was true. I was flawed, defective and thoroughly hated by God. This was so terrifying to me that I was determined to rise above all negativism and be worthy and acceptable to God. I tried to kill every negative thought, feeling, desire or temptation before one ever arose in my mind.

I don't think that his word would have had quite the effect on me if my mother had been balanced and centered in truth. She wasn't. She was, however, an extremely powerful woman and somehow discovered that I could be controlled perfectly by fear, and around the age of 12 I was so frightened out of my wits one time that I gave mother my soul. I lived my inner life as I thought my mother would live her inner life. It was destructive beyond comprehension. I tried to feel her feelings, think her thoughts and lived with a subconscious guilt and shame that almost did me in. At the age of 36 I landed in the hospital with the diagnosis of cancer. The shock of this experience began to turn me around and I too began to examine my history, my church and the influence it had been in my life, and especially mother. Out of this experience I learned that I had to find a new way to live. I've been working on that new way ever since. The first thing I had to do was break the umbilical cord, and the confrontation that took place between me and mother lasted a decade. It took us to the office of a counselor at a psychiatric hospital in Grand Rapids and it took us both through hell. In the office of a counselor my mother at long last and for the first time in my hearing uttered the words, "I was wrong." Still there were unsatisfied yearnings inside of me and about a year and a half before she died in 1983 I asked her if she would verbalize the words "I am sorry," if she could say those words honestly. Her response to me was "I am very sorry. I know I caused your cancer."

Out of this experience I found a new God. I wished at various places when I read your story that you could have touched the real, authentic affirming people that I found in the ecumenical movement especially in the Episcopal and Presbyterian mainline churches. People with class. Real honest class. The books written by Agnes Sanford and Emily Gardner Neal who conveyed the awe and mystery of God opened up a totally different faith and God and little by little my faith has sorted itself out.

Currently, I'm working on my own masters degree in counseling. I especially want to help those who have been "hurt by the church" and there are so many of us. I was encouraged by the final paragraph of your book. I see an open door, somehow, a wide open door. I believe that one day you can invite a different God into your life again. The God I know has taken away my belief that I don't know quite as much as anybody else knows and as a result allowed myself to be walked on, despising myself and the other person also, and has created an individual who refuses to be a scapegoat for anyone and thus I don't need another individual to be my scapegoat. I don't use people as objects; nor will I allow anyone to use me as an object. This miracle occurred as God showed me what I needed to know and see and then gave me what I needed to do to bring about change.

I'm sure this all seems a bit tepid and pale because it's my experience and the experiences that are forceful and bright have to be our own.

Your book doesn't directly tell us about Shirley Ann or the three individuals that call you dad. I assume you have remarried and have stepchildren. Perhaps you will introduce to those of us who read your story thus far more about these individuals in your next book. I'm excited about the next chapter in your life. You are open to truth and life and as they say in twelve step programs, more will be revealed to you. I have no doubt.

As for myself, let me close by saying that I'm going to pray continually that if I ever am allowed to be a therapist and counselor, I won't be filling my counsel with pious platitudes, cliches, truisms, scripture texts, trite advice or admonitions to think more positively. Nor do I think scolding is effective. And no one ever conquered fear when someone tried to scare it out of them. But I'll offer to walk with those who need a companion who find it so dark as they walk through the night because I've found experientially that dawn does follow the night if death doesn't take place in the darkness. Unmerited favor! It's the heart of the good news and missed by so many. My parents never really grasped it. But I'm excited when I think of the opportunity I have to *be* grace, to treat others the way they need to learn to treat themselves. Thank you so much for writing your story. I trust a measure of healing has occurred as you have owned the pockets of darkness (by darkness I mean unawareness, not evil) within you and by owning them, you were empowered to bring these pockets into the light. You will be rewarded by the continual release of more and more understanding and awarenesses. I'm excited about what God is going to do for you as you continue to reclaim your life. It was the will of God for you all along.

Very Sincerely,

Fran Myers

This astute reader proved to be the only one who noticed the significance of the acknowledgment of Shirley Ann in the beginning of *Don't Call Me Brother*.

With extraordinary love, Shirley picked up the pieces of a life that had been shattered by the church of Jesus Christ. With a loving heart, she managed to put them back together. This project took more than love, it took stamina.

Shirley knew that I came with a lot of baggage. The intense love I felt for Rose Marie dominated me. It looked as though I would never get over my divorce, even though it would have been utterly hopeless to expect a reconciliation.

I was filled with anger, even rage, over the lies fed me by the Christian church. By believing those lies and outrageous Christian claims I had lost everything. I winced every time I thought of the stupidity of joining in the singing of the evangelical theme song "I Surrender All" while the Christians skillfully manipulated my life and tore apart my family. With those thoughts constantly in my mind, I had become moody and morose. Rumors about me, instigated by the Christians, circulated everywhere. And as if that wasn't enough, I was still being harassed by the FBI. I had no money or security, a doubtful future, and my health had begun to fail. I was the ideal suitor to take home to mother.

I knew Shirley Ann for four years before I ever asked her for a date. We met in a little church in Cape May Point, New Jersey, during my madness as an evangelist. As I became acquainted with her, many things impressed me. Refreshingly, she did not exhibit the usual traits of a typical pentecostal. She acted like a lady and possessed a genuine sweet spirit. A quiet dignity showed that she had respect for herself. The sincerity of her belief in God could not be disputed. Unlike most church-going people, she was not playing games. I liked her honesty. As an added bonus, she was deliciously attractive, with blonde hair and a trim figure. Her pretty face, with its big eyes and mischievous mouth, could instantly turn impish with a slight twitch of a corner of her mouth or the subtle arching of an eyebrow. A little red applied to her cheeks and nose, a black tear line under her luminous eyes, and a battered top hat with a long-stemmed sunflower rising from the brim would have completed the transformation.

When we finally began to date, the Christians rose to the occasion to try and stop a possible relationship from developing. A close friend (?) in the ministry, whom I really liked, advised me that since I was divorced I would have to live a celibate life. Otherwise, I would displease God. That night this same minister went home and snuggled up to his wife in a warm bed. It's easy to give such advice under those conditions.

Countless interfering Christians, whose advice had not been sought, informed me that "seeing Shirley would ruin my testimony to God." Clearly, love, or even the possibility of love, had no place in the church of Jesus Christ.

Finally, I packed up Shirley and carted her off on a circus tour, away from the meddlesome church people, so that we could work out our own life. The circus people, the non-born-agains, family-oriented as they were, supported us all the way. When we did get married, the "worldly" people were delighted.

Shirley Ann brought into my life a wonderful supportive family. The package came complete with two stepsons, Shawn and Michael, Michael's wife Cindy, and a step-poodle named Deputy. We have also adopted a cross-eyed cat named Kitty Bleu, who loves classical music. Michael helped us to move into a lovely house, and Shirley has proved to be an excellent homemaker.

There are depths to this marriage that go far beyond what I experienced in my previous one. I am also far more protective of this marriage. It is extremely difficult for anyone, especially a Christian, to enter the inner circle of our life. Those who do run the risk of losing a good portion of their head should they attempt (even slightly) to bring any dissent into our marriage. Shirley also left the church after being hurt by the born-agains, and is in total agreement with my views and actions.

My recovery from cancer was just short of a miracle. The phenomenal love from Shirley and the family gave me the supernatural strength I needed to assure that outcome. After the surgery, my doctor said, "I am not surprised. With the love you have around you, and your positive attitude, we knew you would be a quick recovery." Had I continued to live under Christian influence, the result would have been different.

VI

Shout It Out

X These things have I written unto you concerning them that seduce
you.

1 John 2:26

October 30, 1989

Dear Mr. Miles:

I have just finished reading your book *Don't Call Me Brother*
& am extremely pleased & happy that someone gathered
enough nerve to expose these people. I truly would like to
shake your hand. My thoughts have gathered since childhood & I've wished many times that the truth would come
out. I, at this time, am 70 years old which I believe is long
enough to form an opinion. You see, in my own people came
the confusion, when too small to come to any conclusion.
There are too many sheep & they are ripe and open for
the taking. At the same time, us taxpayers are having to
subsidize them, while they turn their noses up at us, in their
judgment of us, seeing us as dirt under their feet. I have
the feeling they lose all guilt & within themselves, they can
do no wrong. I don't want to get carried away because it's
a long, long story.

I do think, if someone, possibly you, could take from
where you left off in your book & write another book from
there, to the grass roots of these people, with a picture that

no one could deny, something could be done. I'm possibly saying too much, Sir, but please be advised, here is one person who takes his hat off to you.

You spoke of working in Michigan State. I kept wondering when I was going to read of one Willie Atwell who had a church in Detroit for many years. Willie died approx. three years ago at around 80 years old. He left Western Kentucky many years ago for Detroit. I was told he did very well with a fine home & drove an upper class car. The big grain in my craw with him was when he had a meeting going on near his home in Kentucky while his nine year old son lay sick with blood poisoning. He finally relented to the pressures of his mother (my grandmother) & took him to the hospital where the child only lived six hours. At this time his body was rotten with gangrene. It wasn't long after this until he went to Detroit. I've always wondered how many deaths he might have caused indirectly, of the very young & old who couldn't help themselves. I would appreciate very much if you did happen to know him & would comment. His widow still lives in Detroit. So the story went, he became neglectful of her at one time, which seemed to follow your pattern in your book. It's a sad feeling knowing that those in the family with the same religion forgave him, and even some who didn't profess any religion. As I say, there are too many sheep. In later years when he was going blind, he availed himself to doctors & the hospital for cornea transplant, of which I understood didn't take. I called it retribution, which was a small price to pay for the life of such a fine specimen as his child. Thank you Mr. Miles & will appreciate hearing from you.

Sincerely,

James H. Atwell
Manchester, Wash.

I have no personal knowledge of Rev. Willie Atwell. In response to my request to reprint his letter, Mr. Atwell gave me some additional information. He started by writing: "Please feel free to use my previous letter & this one also in your writings. It's the best

I can do for a child who lives in his grave from not being old enough to speak for himself when his life was in the balance." Mr. Atwell then told the story of how his grandfather (Rev. Atwell's father) lay sick with pneumonia. In those days, pneumonia was much more difficult to treat and spelled almost certain death. For several days the elder Mr. Atwell dangled between life and death by only a fine thread of hope. Family members took turns sitting with him around the clock, regularly administering the critically required medication that might save his life. When it came time for young Rev. Atwell to sit with his father, he tossed the medication in the coal bucket. The horrified family discovered this the next morning and forbade him to sit with his father again.

Rev. Willie Atwell fits the profile I have developed of the Pentecostal Doctrine-Enforcement Officer perfectly. His practice of spiritual law and medicine caused the death of his little boy, almost killed his father, and as his nephew asks: "Who else?" Yet, while profiting from his "have faith in God" message, Rev. Atwell ran to the doctor the moment he experienced a medical problem of his own. This is not uncommon.

Kenneth Copeland, whose "faith ministry" is well known, is one of many who delude their supporters into believing that they can have anything that they ask God for in faith, "unwavering faith." Copeland successfully preaches a "name-it-and-claim-it" push-button God, and reaps a fortune by promising God's miraculous intervention and healing. I shall now take this opportunity to publicly ask Rev. Copeland to explain his hush-hush trip to Oral Roberts University for that hernia operation. In the meantime, of course, he'll want you to keep those dollars coming in—buy a faithbuilding tape . . . or two or three. . . .

The time is long overdue to take action against these faith healers who have been turned loose on an unsuspecting public. For a starter, there is a law against practicing medicine without a license. Let's demand that district attorneys and prosecutors enforce it. That law was put on the books to protect the public from just this kind of quackery. Labeling it "religion" and "religious freedom" cannot skirt this law. It is the good of the public that is at stake.

Who could forget the spectacle that took place during a "Heritage Today" camp meeting telecast during the early part of 1990? A certain woman preacher walked down to a member of the audience who was hooked up to an oxygen tank with tubes up her nose. After offering a grandstanding healing prayer, the "anointed one" pronounced the woman healed—then yanked the tubes out of her nose. The sick woman began gasping for breath and collapsed. They quickly hooked her back up. The woman evangelist returned to her place behind the pulpit and arrogantly announced that the victim simply did not have enough faith—and went on with her preaching!

"Heritage Today," a spin-off of the aborted PTL Club, like its predecessor, beamed out of Charlotte, North Carolina. During December 1989, the program aired a series of "crisis" telecasts. They needed one million dollars by the end of the month, or that would be the end of them. Indeed, to hear them tell it, the end of *all* Christian televison. On December 8, 1989, in the midst of this million-dollar plea, Rev. Steven Munsey, a pastor of the Family Christian Center in Griffith, Indiana, and a regular guest-host on "Heritage Today," suddenly "spoke under the inspiration of the Holy Spirit": "God has just spoken to me, and told me to tell all people out there with *cancer*, to call the number on the screen . . . Yes, that's right, anyone with cancer, call this number, God will heal you. God just put this on my heart!" Roly-poly Phillip Cameron took the microphone and said, "Yes, send money to this ministry and God will be able to perform that miracle in your life." They continued for five minutes to promise healing for cancer victims if they would take the first step, by "supporting God's work."

I am not a violent person, but had I been in Charlotte, I would have made a fast trip to that TV studio on Park Road and yanked Rev. Munsey and Rev. Cameron off the set. I may yet get that chance. In an interesting twist of fate, The Heritage Ministries decided to tape their programs in Concord, California, *next door to me,* in the Channel 42 studios. Instead of Mohammed going to the mountain, the mountain came to Mohammed. Upon their arrival in the Bay Area on Wednesday, February 7, 1990, the startled theatrical troup was greeted by a stinging but factual article about their operation that I had written for the *San Francisco Examiner,* complete with a cartoon of money raining down from heaven into the outstretched hands of a praying evangelist. There have been some lively media follow-ups, with more to come. The program continued to hustle the bucks under a new name, "Great Life Today." ("Great Life Today," however, proved not to be—it was taken off the air on June 29, 1990.)

October 1, 1989

Dear Mr. Miles:

Just a note to say "thank you" for your book *Don't Call Me Brother*. We used to watch you on PTL and have been involved with diff. ministries over the years. Your book let us know we were not alone in wondering about some of the things we saw. Your book gave us the freedom to trust our judgment. Thanks!

Your involvement with the Lipizzans gives you a special place in our hearts. My husband and I breed Peruvian Paso horses, descendants of Andalusians. May God bless you in your life.

Sincerely,

Steve and Laurie Charter
Martinez, Calif.

Several letters came from disillusioned, former staff members of the Oral Roberts ministry, all of whom were afraid to go public with their criticisms. Many asked me to assess that gigantic Tulsa operation.

Rev. Thomas E. Trask, the superintendent of the Michigan District of the Assemblies of God, told me how in those early days he caught Oral using a "plant" in a wheel chair who would pop up on Roberts' healing command. The faith healer explained the deception to Rev. Trask this way: "Why, this kind of thing just stimulates faith."

So much nuttiness has been connected to Oral Roberts that it would cause a mental hernia to try to reason why anyone would ever take him seriously, much less give him money. Who could forget his soul-stirring promulgation in 1987 that God would "take him home" if his followers didn't send him 8.5 million dollars for the Oral Roberts University scholarship fund. Here are two little known but pertinent facts about that particular drama staged by the Roberts Family Players. Oral said that he would go up to the Prayer Tower, to wait and pray. If the 8.5 mil did not come in on time, he would be "transformed" from there. In the meantime, as verified by the postmaster of Tulsa, the "Victory" letters proclaiming the successful raising of the money were already prepared, stuffed, and ready to mail *before* the "anointed one" climbed to the top of the tower to "await his fate." Oral Roberts knew his flock. After raising the 8.5 million dollars, Rev. Roberts discontinued the scholarship fund that a frantic God supplied the muscle to raise. Where did that money go?

Arlington, Tex.
October 9, 1989

Dear Mr. Miles:

Loved your honest, forthright book!! I realize how hard it must have been to "bare your soul" and admit the truth about the "con game"! The "seven devices" said it all. It is satanic, to say the least.

There are a lot of emotionally weak people attracted to the "fascist-type" environment of these churches. I have always called it a personality/character deficit. Their only way of feeling ½ way decent is to play the game and pay emotionally, physically, and financially.

They should concentrate their efforts on helping the hungry and homeless. Also orphans and single parents. True Christianity is being humble, *generous* and moral. Helping someone and telling *no one* at all is the biggest thrill of all!

I should know! I am an orphan, who grew up in a Presbyterian home (no fanatics, thank God!) and have made a wonderful, successful life for myself. Religion was *never shoved* down my throat, while living at the home. They knew the boundaries. Hope you write another book. Hope to see you on the talk show circuit. I always enjoy your appearance.

Best Wishes
Mrs. C.A.

Columbia, Md.
October 6, 1989

Austin Miles
c/o Prometheus Books

Dear Sir:

It took me about three months to find your book, about three days to read it. I just "happened" to hear your voice on my radio dial one Sunday morning on my way home from work, and recognized you, on an interview discussing your problems with publication. I am in the process now of wrapping it to send to the only other person I know strong enough to handle it, my former pastor.

I pray by this time you have found a renewed zeal for Christ, in your own way, and will keep your eyes on Jesus this time, not on men. God forbid that you should be responsible for the offense of any as so many were to you. (Matt. 18:6, does this not also include the "young" or new believers? I think it does.)

There are still many independent Pentecostal churches in the country, as well as the non-denominational "charismatic" churches which have sprung up in recent years. While none of us and therefore none of the churches which we comprise are perfect, there are nonetheless good Christians everywhere. The Assembly of God is NOT the body of Christ, or the "bride of Christ," only faithful forgiven Christians will make up that spotless church. It does seem to be the humble servants in the background who are best able to withstand the temptations of the world.

Speaking of temptations, did you know the silver-tongued Irish Bob Gass, who so gleefully dismissed you as "Mr. Miles," left his big, beautiful Glad Tidings church in Bangor, Maine, under a cloud of scandal after confessing to sexual indiscretion with one of his parishioners? Many of the church members there remember it well.

I am sorry for Jim Bakker, Jimmy Swaggart, and the rest, but I feel worse yet for the many new, unestablished Christians who fell with them. Even Christian idols have clay feet, that's why Jesus is the only solid foundation.

In closing, don't ever doubt that God loves you and holds a unique place of ministry for you. Study the Word and hold fast to that which he has given you. God bless you, YOU ARE SPECIAL!!!

Yours Truly,

Mrs. C.S.

Rev. Bob Gass, a former PTL Club favorite, did a lot of damage to the cause of Jesus Christ by an adulterous episode that he finally confessed to. He is currently a part of the ministry of Bishop Earl Paulk of the Chapel Hill Harvester Church in Decatur, Georgia. During an appearance on "The Larry King Show," where Bishop Paulk had come to dispute me and my book, a caller pointed out that the bishop had been kicked out of his former denomination, The Church of God, over the same charge, adultery. Bishop Paulk admitted the indiscretion, then said: "This is why I can be so effective in helping to restore ministers and be compassionate. I've been there myself and know the pain."

September 16, 1989

Dear Austin Miles:

Recently I listened to you and your story when you were a guest on Ray Appleton's radio talk show, on KMG Fresno (California). On that very day I checked and found your book *Don't Call Me Brother* to be out of stock in the bookstores in Fresno, but last week fortunately it was again available. I have read it cover to cover, and some parts twice and three times again. I can certainly relate to your story. I, too, am a "survivor" of the charismatic fundamentalist movement.

Although I am still a young man (thirty-four) and my own experience did not involve consequences of the depth and magnitude that you yourself endured, I certainly did not emerge totally unscathed. In many, many aspects I am deeply mentally scarred, and did suffer estrangement from my family for some time, which certainly does not seem to go along well with all the "love" that I was supposed to have been experiencing.

My own personal experience involved spending nearly two years with a non-denominational group of "Jesus people" in Eureka, California, in 1972–1974. The organization was called Gospel Outreach, and was Pentecostal in nature. We even went so far as to recognize among ourselves *Apostles*, men of the church who were led by God to act in the very same capacity as Christ's apostles during His lifetime. Our group practiced fundamentalist teachings to the letter, including Baptism in the Holy Spirit, shunning of dissenters, proselytizing, and remaining separate from non-Christians except in necessary business and witnessing. During that time and subsequently I had fellowship with various established denominations including Assemblies of God.

To say that what I did was not that of a "cult" is to deny simple open-faced fact.

For several years after departing from Gospel Outreach I continued to try to live as a disciple of Christ, but today I live as a man chained to no one particular mind-set. I still retain my personal regard for high moral character in my fellow human being, but do not believe that it is at all necessary to be a "born again" Christian in order to lead a completely upright, morally correct, and satisfying, fulfilling life. For those who do believe this way, I say "more power to you" but leave me and my neighbors out of your heavenly plans.

It is also a tragedy that you should have been made to suffer such persecution at the hands of an office of the United States government. Too many people are given way too much power in the name of law and order, justice, national security, and so on. Why democracy needs to resort to such non-democratic principles and tactics as those the FBI and other investigative offices of the U.S. government have been known to employ, will probably always remain a mystery to my mind. I truly hope you are now free of such harassment, and that some day a way will be found to prevent this from occurring to other innocent persons.

In conclusion, I applaud you for your tremendous inner

strength that you drew upon to help yourself through those terrible times, and I wish you now continued success with your career and new family. And if you're in the Fresno area sometime in the future, please let your presence be known. I would truly enjoy meeting you in person. And please excuse my handwriting mistakes and corrections, but a typewritten letter just wouldn't have been right.

Once again, the best of fortune to you and your family.

Sincerely Yours,

Forrest R. Prince
Selma, Calif.

October 12, 1989

Dear Mr. Miles:

I have just finished *Don't Call Me Brother* and I feel like I've lost a friend. I so looked forward to reading the book that I tried not to read too much at one sitting.

Your life has been, needless to say, incredible, and a testament to your courage. I cried during your account of how Rose Marie left and I seethed with anger when you described how the various church bodies persecuted you. I could relate personally to your early life—my father divorced my mother when I was twelve and I, too, was alone most of my childhood since my mother worked and my sister, six years my senior, married at age 20 and moved across the country. I, too, searched for a place to belong and I, too, said the sinner's prayer—when I was fourteen. Unfortunately, I, too, have found that churches are not always the safe havens they appear to be. I have done research on various cults and religious movements.

The book is particularly poignant as we have recently learned of the Bakkers' conviction, despite the fact that they continue to believe they are "innocent in God's eyes" and continue to have a multitude of followers.

I have not lost my faith, but I am very wary of those claiming to be "born again." I care deeply for many beautiful

people who are not Christian and I have a hard time believing these people are headed for Hell. ~~I believe that the
world will eventually have one faith, one God and that people will eventually stop killing and hurting each other in
the name of God.~~ Aren't all religions simply looking at different parts of the "elephant"?

If you are making any appearances in the Orange County
area, I would be honored to meet you. There are many
questions I'd like to ask.

Sincerely,

Warren Beacon
Orange, Calif.

In response to my request to print his letter, Warren excitedly
scribbled me a letter dated December 3, 1989. He stated that he
was writing to me in the early morning of his wedding day. "I'm
marrying the same woman who I married 10 years ago, then divorced almost 2 years ago. We've come so far. We realized in our
separation, that we still love each other enough to work at it again."
Now this is the kind of news I love to hear. *Congratulations!*

Willowdale, Ontario, Canada
August 7, 1989

Dear Mr. Miles:

I have just completed your book *Don't Call Me Brother*, and
am taking the liberty of contacting you through your
publisher.

I found your book to be refreshingly well written and
honest and I congratulate you upon it. One of the 10 books
I have written and which have been published in a number
of foreign languages and editions was the biography of
Oswald J. Smith, the founder of The Peoples Church. Like
you I got too close and like you I "lost God in church."
Realizing that you can't beat them my wife and I left the
organized church and haven't been back in over 10 years.

We've never been happier.

Again, congratulations on having the strength to tell your story. I am sure that in spite of the backlash and pressures from the Assemblies of God there will be more people who believe you than not.

Yours Sincerely,

Douglas Hall

Bryan, Ohio
February 5, 1990

Dear Austin:

I checked out your book from the library this past week and started reading it this morning. I could barely set it down and I finished it this evening.

I was so affected by what I read that I not only discussed it with my husband but also with my lady friend over the telephone.

You see, I have also had some very bad experiences with some Christians. I could go on about them, but I don't feel it's necessary. What has happened since is more important. I decided (slowly) to steer away from anything that was unreasonable or did not make sense. I am still a Christian, but I stay away from a lot of organized religion, and I only do what I feel is right. I guess I am very fortunate in that respect. At one point in my life I was very vulnerable, and I believe that my husband and the Lord protected me from all the bad aspects of today's "Christianity."

I used to be very bitter about my experiences, but I am slowly learning to let go of them. I am also very careful of whom I associate with. My circle of friends includes Christian people and non-Christian people, and I treasure them all. I don't, however, tend to associate with those who would like to run my life. My life is in the hands of God, not some evangelist who wants every dime I have.

I have been, to some extent, very skeptical about some

of these TV preachers. After reading your book, I am even more skeptical. It confirmed some of my previous feelings and/or suspicions. I realize a lot of damage has been done in "the name of Jesus" to a lot of people over the years, and it pains me. I told my husband tonight, "I wonder if God looks down on all this and just shakes his head."

I sincerely hope and pray that you return to our Lord someday with more "street-smarts" about "religion."

Sincerely,
P.F.

APO Miami, Fla.
November 11, 1989

Dear Mr. Miles:

I would just like to take this opportunity to thank you for your recent book entitled, *Don't Call Me Brother*. It touched me so deeply that I felt very compelled to write to you as a personal admirer. I've never written a letter like this before and I'm not a very creative writer, so what I'll try to do is write what's in my heart. All I ask with all due respect, is that you bear with me and hear what I have to say.

First of all, allow me to introduce myself and give you a little background. My name is Alfredo Perez, I'm 32 years old, I have a lovely wife and two darling daughters, and I am currently serving in the U.S. Air Force in Panama while my family is staying back home in Southern California. I am also a believer in Jesus Christ; however, I'm not at all associated with any denomination and I'm currently studying to some day be a pastor/teacher after my service career.

I must say that after reading your book with great interest, I became very saddened and very angry at the same time. It was sad because of everything that has happened to you in your life. The anger is for the treachery of the Assemblies of God and the evil that was done to you. I've had my own dealings with the religious organizations of today. Allow me to share some of it with you.

I was married once before to a young woman who did

so much cheating on me that I lost count during those terrible three years. Finally in late 1982, we decided to get a divorce. I was extremely heartbroken, but quite fortunately, we had no children between us, which made the divorce proceedings a lot less complicated. About four days later, I was driving my car around town with really nowhere to go. I just fell apart and started crying. It was at that point that I asked God that if He would help me straighten my life out, I would follow and serve Him. Later that night, a friend from work asked me if I wanted to go out with this nice young woman that he knew for a simple luncheon date. Although I was a little hesistant toward his suggestion due to my recent divorce, I accepted. My friend told me that she was real religious and had gone through a similar divorce herself a year and a half earlier. After a quite successful date, we continued together until we got married in August 1983. I must admit, she never pushed her Christianity on me, except just simply inviting me to church when I felt comfortable. Out of respect for her, I started going with her almost immediately until I finally did ask Jesus to come into my heart in early 1983. When we got married, she moved up from Santa Ana and Riverside to an apartment we rented in San Bernardino, California.

We were attending a large Southern Baptist church and wanted to get married there, but the pastor refused on account of our divorces. We had to get the local Air Force chaplain to marry us at her parents' house there in town. After we got married, we proceeded to go ahead and officially join that church. Things for us there started pretty smoothly until about the beginning of 1986. The church hired a teacher from the Southern Baptist Convention in Dallas that specialized in tithing, for about $5,000.00. Then the church started a monthly pledge program in which the people would make a promise to God to pay so much a month for three years in order to raise a cool ten million dollars for the purchase of property and larger church facilities. I guess that all sounded innocent enough, except for the fact that the Bible never taught anyone to give by compulsion or by signing anything. This doesn't even include the fact that they indoctrinate you into having to do something for God every day, such as witnessing, visitations, socials, home Bible studies, and anything else they can come up with to occupy your week, away from your family. I began to question a lot of their activities and even some of their teachings. One thing I struggled with was that the Southern Baptists teach that the gifts of the Spirit was done away with in the first century. I couldn't find any such evidence in the Bible. They were also into rebaptizing people who did not originally get baptized in their church, also not of God's Word. Tithing was a major problem. *We "tithed" our ten percent to the church while we had to use our Mastercard to pay for our normal house bills* [emphasis mine]. Something was definitely wrong, either on God's part or on the church's. I began to take courses in Biblical Greek to see if the original languages held an answer for me. To my amazement, there were lots of words in the Bible that were not correctly translated into English.

Finally in January 1987, we left the Baptist Church and found a small non-denominational church in Redlands that strictly taught the Bible from both the Greek and the Hebrew. This interested me very much in my spirit. I went ahead and took Hebrew language and customs courses so that I could familiarize myself with the Jews and their ways. After all, there is no denying that Jesus was a Jew. I was astonished at what I started learning in the Bible, looking at it from the Hebrew instead of American perspective. Things are totally different between Americans and Jews, many ways of doing things being totally opposite from us.

Allow me to share with you what I've learned and my personal feelings towards what has happened to you. First of all, let me assure you that being a Christian does not mean being a member of Assemblies of God, the Southern Baptists, the Catholics, or anyone else. Being a Christian or believer means being repentant over your sins and having Jesus Christ come into your life, to change you to what He's asked you to be. If there is no change, there is no repentance, therefore no salvation. It is a very personal thing, not something derived from any organization from earth. I can't stand what is known as religion today because many people have been either emotionally or physically destroyed in the name of organized religion. You see, my wife and

I used to watch Paul and Jan on TBN along with all their frenzied friends performing all sorts of "signs and wonders." We also watched Jim and Tammy Bakker, Jimmy Swaggart, Oral and Richard Roberts; now there's a fine pair. Like Father, like son. What kills me is that these people, with all the falsehood that they have, are about as fearful of God as I am when I walk across a yard of grass. No, I don't hate any of these people; however, there is no way that I agree with most everything they do. You see, God asked us to be doers of His Word, not just sayers. And the greatest way to witness to the world about Christ is not to make a fool of yourself at work or on the streets, but to walk in such a manner and to conduct your whole life in such a way that it radiates Christ through you. It doesn't mean that we won't make our usual daily mistakes because, after all, we're all human. Christ has already paid the price for our fumblings, but it doesn't excuse us from seriously trying to live right. Unfortunately, organized religion is nothing but big business these days. In contrast to how you finished your book, I can assure you that Christ's true bride is without spot or blemish. If by any chance they were once Christians in the past, then for them, the falling away is definitely in progress.

If you recall Matthew 7:21–23, Jesus said, "Not everyone who says to Me, 'Lord, Lord' will enter the kingdom of heaven; but he who *does* the will of My Father who is in heaven. Many will say to Me on that day, 'Lord, Lord, did we not prophesy in Your Name, and in Your Name cast out demons, and in Your Name perform many miracles?' And then I will declare to them, I never knew you; depart from Me, you who practice lawlessness." In other words, Mr. Miles, saying "spiritual" things like PRAISE THE LORD, GLORY TO GOD, AMEN, HALLELUJAH, and so forth does not make anybody a Christian. A true personal relationship with Jesus Christ is your salvation, nothing more and nothing less.

These people you were involved with used you while you didn't buck the system. Once you started rocking the boat, they decided to take pot shots on you and yours. I say that you should definitely be angry at what they've done to you. Therefore, let them receive much blame from you, but please don't blame God. The Lord has given everyone a free will to either use it according to His Word, or destructively pervert it. These people chose to be self-righteous and evil. And God cannot go back on His Word and interfere in how Man wants to conduct himself. I can assure you of one thing, these people are *not* Christians in any sense of the word and they are not brothers and sisters of mine. *Our pastor is well aware with what they're made of. He graduated from an Assemblies college in San Diego. After graduation, he turned around and gave the diploma back to the school. When they asked why, he told them that he didn't learn anything in the Bible, but simply how to manipulate innocent people and make money off of them* [emphasis added].

We at our church are always under attack by other churches, especially Assemblies of God. These are the false prophets and teachers that Jesus warned us about throughout His Gospels. I mean, let's face it, false religions like Hinduism and Satanic cults are obvious, but wouldn't the devil profit more if he attacked from inside the church? You bet. To put it mildly, Christianity as the world sees it, is a joke. Therefore, I've learned to really never trust any man with my life, just God. He really is the Way, the Truth, and the Life, not Brother "Z," Jim and Tammy, Oral, or any others in this brood of vipers. Believe me when I tell you, Mr. Miles, that these people will pay for what they've done to you. Nobody is above God's Word, and the actions of these people condemned themselves. Oh, how much that I feel your grief at the losses of your Rose Marie and Lori. I just wish there was something, anything, I can do to help you get them back. Be somewhat relieved in knowing that God is allowing them to drop like flies in scandal. Jim Bakker recently got 45 years in jail; sometimes I feel that just isn't enough for the permanent damage they've caused to many. I know in my heart, however, that God's Wrath has not stopped here, but has only begun. You know why so many innocent people get sucked up into all this? It's because most are actually too lazy to study the Bible themselves, so they can't recognize the enemy.

Anyway, I thank you so much, Mr. Miles, for letting me pour my heart out to you. I know that many years ago you really made an honest commitment to God. I am also aware that a group of religious leaders and liars won a battle over you by destroying most of you, but I assure you that they have not won the war. Be angry at them, but please don't be angry at God. He still loves you now just as much as when you were in the ministry. As a matter of fact, the very person that "witnessed" to you caused your very downfall with the Assemblies of God. He should have never told you to "proudly" carry your Bible to and fro. That doesn't prove a thing. The Assemblies should have never coerced you to leave show business to go into a "ministry." There's nothing wrong with being a ringmaster/narrator. I think it is a wonderful thing to do, and I'm glad you went back to it. For some reason, a lot of Christians today think that in order to be a "good Christian," you always have to get "into the ministry." Some of the greatest ministries in the world are in normal, everyday jobs. I still believe that you are truly my brother, not these other wackos of life. I implore you not to give Him up, and for some reason my spirit tells me that you really haven't. I just want you to know that if you ever need to talk to a person who really cares, talk to me. Find somewhere where there are true believers, especially in normal, non-controlled, Bible-believing churches. They're out there, but they're definitely far and few between. Mind you we're not perfect, but we sure try. Once again, thank you very much for sharing your life; it is something that I will always treasure in my heart. Please allow me to leave you with this: May He who is the Lord grant you peace that surpasses all understanding and may you, once again, find a place in your heart for Him. God bless you always.

Yours very sincerely,

Alfredo B. Perez

VII

Gifts Without Repentance

For the gifts and calling of God are without repentance.

Romans 11:29

Tulsa, Okla.
September 18, 1989

Dear Mr. Miles:

Certainly *Don't Call Me Brother* is a horror story of the first magnitude. In view of all you suffered at the hands of people who professed not only to be Christians, but people in the front ranks of Christian leadership, it is easy to see why you succumbed to discouragement, bitterness and cynicism.

My wife and I have suffered some from mistakes made by Christian leadership. Our experiences, however, were mild compared to the onslaught which you went through. I believe that the only thing that enabled us to receive healing from our experiences was the comfort which God himself provided directly to us, although we did receive comfort from some understanding Christians as well.

I believe that only the direct ministry of Jesus to you will bring the true comfort you need, and I pray that you will receive that comfort. In your book you indicate that you even came to the point of doubting God's existence. Doesn't the fact that you still recognize the goodness in Ben Kinchlow and in the late Aubrey Sara demonstrate the reality of God and his intervention in our world? You know that both Ben and Aubrey would be quick to deny that the goodness within them came from themselves. Unless these men have been deceived, the love reflected in their lives comes from Jesus Christ alone.

In your book you correctly indict hypocrisy and spiritual pride (in both of which, I'm sorry to say, I have at times participated). When we don't live according to the Bible, we obviously cause people to question its validity. The "Commentary" is wrong, however, when it attempts to prove that the New Testament doesn't encourage a Christian to love his unsaved wife. Is it really too "mystical" to relate a husband's love for his wife (saved or not) to that of Christ for His Church? Obviously that love should be so strong that we would sacrifice our own selfish interests for their growth, encouragement and protection. Also, what of Eph. 5:29–31? This certainly doesn't suffer from the "mystical" objection.

I can certainly understand that you must feel that your entire Christian life was a mistake, and I will make the assumption that if you had never become a Christian you would have lived a perfectly "happy" life with Rose Marie. What would have happened to you after you died? If truly you have been saved and are destined to spend eternity with Jesus Christ, have you made a bad bargain by losing earthly happiness? See 1 Cor. 15:19.

If you followed me around you would no doubt see (although hopefully on a smaller scale than set forth in the book) hypocrisy, coldness, self-indulgence, unbelief, and spiritual pride. I say this to my shame, but not to the shame of the One who bought me with His blood. I know that I've only tasted a small portion of His goodness, but I can say that such goodness is beyond anything that you and I could imagine in a thousand millennia of imaginings.

The following may sound hollow or pious to you, but don't give up on Jesus or on the book which He dictated. By the way, did you know that when God gives gifts and callings He doesn't take them back? Rom. 11:29.

Sincerely yours,

G.B.

June 23, 1989

Dear Austin,

I read with interest your book *Don't Call Me Brother.*

I agree with much of what you have said because I know it's true. I believe God has called you to be a part of His ministry and I believe you should not worry about opinions from others, but should be back out ministering to those that need the love, help, & understanding that you are capable of. Too many pastors, ministers and evangelicals are fleecing the flock.

I do hope that some of those who have fallen away from God, such as Jim Bakker, will find their way back.

God Bless You,

You have a friend in Kansas City.

Your brother in Christ,

Larry Dashner

P.S. I'm sorry over the sadness you have felt over the past years as a servant of Jesus.

Dear Austin,

I am writing you this letter because I have a message for you. In every system God put someone in the system to break the system. You are the one that God put in the system. How do you break the system? By not going along with it. You will be challenged to do something that is wrong and against your system. Stand up for right and God will be with you. This is the time to stand up and be counted.

God's plan is for everyone. To experience the good way and the bad way then choose which way you want to go. The good way promises you nothing and gives you everything. Freedom. The other way promises you everything and gives you nothing but despair. God is for everyone. The other way benefits no one. God knows you can do it. You have been tested many times and have come through for good ways. God knows there is good teachings mixed in with bad teachings that we are confused. That is why he sends a guardian angel when we are in a bind.

We know that fear knocks out God and this is what will be used on you. When you feel this coming on Ask for God's help. He will send help from above. A guardian angel.

You will be opening the door for good ways to come in and the young to come in and help. They are strong in God and will show us the way.

He will be rooting for you to come through. We love you for hanging in there when the going got tough. As the saying goes, when the going gets tough, the tough get going.

God Bless You & Take Care.

With love

A. C.
Chester, Vt.

October 17, 1989
Harrisburg, Pa.

Dear Austin Miles,

I am very sorry for you that you had your eyes on men. Men will let you down a lot of the time. Men let God down too. But He keeps loving us anyway. If you could get through to the spirit of religion & as The Bible talks about, false teachers, etc., and people in general and actually ask yourself: What has God ever done to hurt me?

I, myself, have had some close encounters with The Lord. I have seen a burning flame as big as a person, not burning any thing, in answer to a prayer. I have seen other visions, etc. My relationship with God has been give & take—I mostly take, & He mostly gives. I hope I can some way change that, as I move upward in the getting to know my Lord through His word. None of us want to move backward.

As far as you getting involved in The Assemblies of God Church—that is a denomination—God never had one—what denomination is Billy Graham?—You do not have to be affiliated with a denomination and their hang-ups & man-made doctrines in order to know, love & serve God. Don't let Satan blind you, you're smarter than that. Just cause people let you down, doesn't give you an excuse to turn your back on Almighty God. He still loves you. Praying for you always—as—*none of us are perfect.*

Love,

Paula Powell

Sunday, October 22, 1989

Dear Sir,

I read your book, *Don't Call Me Brother,* and also the book *Salvation For Sale,* not yours; each was fantastic and so exceptionally well put. I always believed organizations had to have accountants & bookkeepers galore to keep track of each penny.

I appreciate so very, very much what it must have taken to write your thoughts, the courage to write about our nation's religious shortcomings, but also your own, very own, personal love story. Few men ever reveal their own love life. Your lady had many wonderful charms, dear, but underneath it all, she was wordly and materialistic. She was, "of the world," as I, too, lean too much in that direction—I do believe much like you and admire you in your strong faith. Each person you & I will ever meet will believe entirely different. I passed both books to a Catholic, dear elderly friend—a most devout, disciplined wonderful lady. She is such a witness & guide to me. I was raised Baptist & later joined Methodist & now stopped going. I do believe in God & He is with me each step I take. I stopped going when we had an election here, small one, & many in my church voted for an admitted drunk. I felt they condoned drinking to do this.

Back to your book—your love story was so personal & precious, but your lady was flawed, as we all are, dear. I was so hurt and appalled how she lured your daughter away from you and your love and how she did it so effortlessly. Your daughter had to have been so weak to be led so easily.

Again, Sir, thank you for opening up your heart to us, your fans. My best to you, forever. You can't ever become a Christian and drop it entirely, I do not believe. You or I may backslide but we can't discard our beliefs entirely.

So I'll say, thanking you from the bottom of my heart, a fellow Christian (not too good of one but one nevertheless). I firmly believe God understands you & me when we don't understand ourselves. Go with God—God Bless! A fan forever—

Mrs. M. D.
Missouri

August 3, 1989
Mexico

Dear Mr. Miles,

Greetings to you from our little family here in Mexico. Trusting this letter will find you well and fruitful in your call as a minister to the circus people.

I had the opportunity to read your book and would like to make some comments. I am aware that you have already received other opinions in regards to your book, perhaps negative, perhaps positive, but it is my desire to share my thoughts anyway, as a Christian sister, trusting that you will hear me out, and that God will use His Holy Spirit to touch you at this most difficult time.

First, I can understand the reasons for writing such a book, to reveal to others some very secretive and important events that are happening in the church today. Things that you experienced, and saw that you feel the public needs to be aware of, and felt it your responsibility to tell them. Many parts of your book were depressing and discouraging, when one realizes that there are people, Christians that you admire, love and respected that have become imperfect in the sense of getting involved in immorality, homosexuality, fraud, etc., but as I continued to read I became more aware of bitterness and resentment that you, dear Mr. Miles, are carrying around in your heart, that needs to be dealt with before it destroys you and your walk with the Lord. What happened to you Mr. Miles isn't so uncommon in the Christian Church. Your case was one of many due to power struggle and unfortunately, politics, that separate the family of God. You must realize that God *always* vindicates the anointed that He intends to use in the ministry, and even more so when this person has been innocently pushed around by his peers. God has taught us to get our eyes off man, they are imperfect and will always cause us to stumble. Do you realize Mr. Miles that there wouldn't be a minister or missionary in the ministry, if all of us made the choice you did? We cannot *give up* because the enemy comes against us! Eph. 6 uses the body of Christ as an example of how important it is to put on the whole armor of God to resist the enemy. Somehow, dear Mr. Miles, you let your armor slip and allowed yourself to become discouraged by what you were seeing and experiencing. In writing your book you are doing exactly what you are against, and many people will read it and not become saved, because they will weigh what you've said, and blame all Christians to be the same. My heart was burdened for you and hurt by the fact that God has an obvious anointing in your life and you have turned your back on that anointing. Do you realize how hard it is to find true, sincere, devout, sold-out ministers that are willing to live by faith and not put a price tag on Christianity?

My husband and I have been missionaries for 20 years in Mexico. We see a great need for ministers in the Mexican Church, people to come down and give their lives to serve Christ as teachers in our school and mission. We have so much work that needs to be done and few willing to go and be obedient to the great commission. Then I read your book and I cried to the Lord. Oh Father, another minister "biting the dust." How come Lord? Is it because of resentment and bitterness that has built up over the years that has not been dealt with and then in the end destroys? Tears filled my eyes as I read the rejection you felt and the hurt. In that moment I stopped and prayed for you: "God fill Mr. Miles with your love once again and help him to realize that you, too, know what it is to suffer rejection, loss of everything, humbled, but you still carried out your ministry even to the end. You didn't give up. Help him to realize the need for ministers that love you, and that will minister to the deep need in the Christian body, knowing that just because one is saved, one isn't without sin."

I just read about a retreat center, R&R resort that perhaps could help you renovate and rededicate your life to God's service. It is a Christian training Center in Franklin, N.C. They deal with pastors that are broken in some way and help them to overcome areas and problems in their life. I do not know of them personally but appreciate their ministry and what they have done for countless missionaries. Pray about this Mr. Miles, maybe God would use Larry and Susan Pons to help you overcome this negative attitude that seems to have overtaken you, and that your book expresses.

I know you are probably asking, "who is this woman that writes this letter?" I want you to know, that my husband and I have been where you are, and know what it is to be rejected and hurt, but God vindicated us and has given us new purpose and vision in our lives to continue serving Him. We are aware that there are alot of Jim Bakkers out there but we have chosen not to allow their testimonies to destroy our service for the Lord. Each person will give account to the Lord, for everything, anyway, so why allow them to destroy what God wants to do through us? We pray for those that walk the crooked path and pray for ourselves that God will help us to keep turning our cheeks, forgiving them 490 times for one offense. There are so few of us out to revolutionize the world for Jesus, that we must keep going on. Jesus needs the faithful! Bear in mind that not all Christians, missionaries, pastors are the same. You cannot weigh what happened to you by everybody. There are some mighty fine and sincere followers of Christ that

truly serve Him with their whole heart. My prayer for you
is that you too will recognize this and return to what God
has called you to do and forgive those that have hurt and
offended you. God will then open up a whole new ministry
for you and it will be far more fruitful than your last.

Remember that there will be trials and tribulations, we
do not live in a garden of roses without splinters. May God
bless you as you read this letter and may you know that
my husband and myself are praying for you that you will
one day return to the ministry. Satan shall be defeated but
only by those who bear the marks, and have learned to be
overcomers.

Bless you, dear Mr. Miles.

Yours in His Service

B. K.

November 21, 1989

Craig Hatcher
2408 Meadow Rue Dr.
Modesto, CA 95355

Mr. Austin Miles
c/o Prometheus Books
700 East Amherst St.
Buffalo, New York 14125

Greetings Austin,

Recently I was returning from a business trip from Bakers-
field to Modesto, California, when I was listening to an
evangelical radio station talk show. The host was discussing
you and your book and had managed to patch you through
on a long distance phone line to answer questions. Generally,
I don't listen to evangelical radio stations (although I was
a Baptist pastor for 7 years and did degreed graduate work
at two seminaries), because often those who minister on

them seem to come from the "wacko" fringe groups of miscast Biblical theology. For some reason I listened with interest to this particular show—to such a degree that I bought your book a couple of weeks ago and read it.

The reading of your book was difficult for me, I read it with great sorrow. It was the sorrow of what had happened to your life and the injustices which you suffered. I, too, suffered from injustices from denominational politics, although not to the degree of your suffering. I gain no pleasure from knowing the sins of other "ministers" of the Gospel, yet sins cannot be hidden, for if they are they only grow unrepentantly and fester all the more.

I gave a great deal of thought to your book and came up with some conclusions, which may or may not be accurate, depending on how well I think I understood what you wrote. First, the God of the Bible is real. He used you to do many works of good and righteousness for others. Second, you had/have value in His usage. More than you realize. God used you in healing ministry (I, too, was healed by Jesus of a permanent disability which came upon me when I was injured in the Marine Corps). Disease has an ugly side to it, as in the death of Lyn. Yet, all disease is not physical.

The insidiousness of spiritual disease is ugly as well. God showed you both of these. He showed you His victory over the disease of the body through the mercy of Christ Jesus. God then showed you the spiritual disease of the church today. He showed it to you in a special way—through personal suffering. You alone do not suffer in this—you lost every thing and still suffer from wounds of the soul. God also suffers with you in this. In a way, this was a gift, although it may not be recognized as such. To see things as God sees them is difficult for the human mind to accept. God allowed you to see how the sins of the church are and to know in your mind and heart how foul these are. This tells me that you indeed love God and His Truth. The opposite of love is not hate, the opposite of love is no longer caring. You care, even through your grievous wounds, you care a great deal. Your anger shows your caring for you have a prophetic anger—an anger against God's people for being willingly deceived.

The corruption which you saw in the Assemblies of God, PTL and elsewhere is historically cyclical. The same has been seen in other quarters of the church throughout history—it is not new, merely better known.

I became a Christian in 1970 in a Baptist church which had become overly charismatic. I saw and experienced truthful workings of the Spirit of God. I also saw short-sighted ministers, "medicine show" teachings, incredibly anti-biblical theology and the root of the problem.

The foulness of some quarters of the church and of certain ministers is the desire for personal power. To maintain this power requires the manipulation of the church members including the manipulation of their purses. The power is maintained by the corrupt minister preaching that the people can also have some of this "power" for their own lives. It is all a self-serving fraud of Christianity. Alas it is very widespread. The minister who fawns to build up his own image as Christ's servant commits ministerial prostitution. The followers who follow men do just that—they divorce themselves from following Christ to follow men and the doctrines of men. You saw this and suffered. You wouldn't "go along with the flow" and paid the price. Through it all God was showing you the truth of the ways of men.

For some reason, pentecostal churches tend to draw unstable people and raise up unstable ministers. It is as if the message of the Man of Galilee is not enough. Hence, He is put aside, and a new gospel comes forth putting the individual before God and in some cases psychologically enslaving them to a power broker minister. It is also unfortunate that these ministers are of high visibility in the public eye. The Mexicans have a proverb—it is the empty jug that makes the most noise.

It would be easy to give up. It would be easy to survey personal wounds and see the gigantic size of the corruption in the church and to say to yourself, "I'm just going to chuck it all and go my own way." Somehow, I don't think that you are that selfish. I really think that your ministry has yet to begin.

Spiritual corruption exists only because of secrecy. If the sins were exposed, brought out into the light, most

Christians, even the "crazed pentecostals" would see and reprove them. Only lies and secrecy can allow corruption to exist and to grow. When ministers crave power (and the money which maintains it through manipulation) corruption will always follow. The personal ego is never sated nor can it be. It is like the flesh—ever hungry and never satisfied. Too often, the Devil is blamed for evil. Surely he is the father of evil, but more often than not, evil can exist in the flesh of men. We often give the Devil more credit than what is due. The flesh cannot be cast out.

I was intrigued by your citing Dr. Cohen. It is true that Christians can become brainwashed—but only when persuaded to submit to an authoritarian minister. A true minister guides his sheep towards the Lordship of Jesus with great patience. He doesn't try to replace the Holy Spirit in the life of the believer. In Christ, the individual has dignity and worth which is holy to God and is not to be manipulated by any minister. Manipulative ministers are weak and operate in the flesh instead of in the Spirit of grace and truth. True ministers try to persuade from the Word and leave the application of the Word to the Holy Spirit. False ministers use the word in error trying to enslave their parishioners. I suppose that the pentecostals are more often guilty of this in that their development of systematic theology is often quite poor, but this is a personal reflection.

I mentioned that your real ministry may not yet have begun. I feel, or suggest, that your real ministry may be that of calling the church back to righteousness, beginning at the top. A church body is usually no better than its leadership. If the leadership is corrupt, all manner of evil will enter into the congregation and victimize it. A real revival is not that which is preached to the church members, but to the church staffs. From them, the reviving will filter down to the congregation.

Should churches be taxed? They could be by law and actually have no constitutional protection against taxation. I feel that taxation would only increase the corruption which already exists. I would suggest that since churches are state sanctioned, that they should also be accountable to the state. The state should have the duty to do an annual audit of the church to see where the funds have been used. With this information in the open, it would be more difficult for corruption to abound and the members would have a clearer vision of where God's money is going. For the churches to have benefits from the state also obligates them to be regulated, at least financially, by the state.

I hope that this letter has not been too rambling and that my insights are not too far off. I am persuaded from your book that your calling from God is but taking a rest and that your best is still to come, after all, You are Special.

In His Service,

Craig

P.S.: I never have preached on tithing or on money. In my first pastorate, I suggested no longer using the collection plate. I felt it was an embarrassment to the poor and people should come to church to receive. The deacons thought I was crazy. Without the collection plate, our offerings quadrupled and we completed two major building programs fully paid for. Money was never sought—the people gave for the right reason—they wanted to. God doesn't need money. Churches need humility—God knows needs and satisfies them.

The writer of this beautiful letter exhibited a rare kind of Christian spirit and attitude that has become all but extinct. I almost feel like King Agrippa saying to the Apostle Paul: "Almost thou persuadest me to be a Christian [again]" . . . Acts 26:27.

I experienced some beautiful moments during my ten years of Christian service that will always remain close to my heart. I soared on mysterious wings of supernatural power during an exhilarating adventure that allowed me to witness and become a part of the authentic workings of God. I have felt the genuine power of God surging through my body when one of the marvelous Gifts of The Holy Spirit manifested itself. There is absolutely nothing on earth to compare to that sensation.

However, the cost involved for these temporary highs was too great. I would never have agreed to sacrifice my family for this experience. Nor would I have knowingly opened myself up to the sort of maniacal, rabid misfits that one finds in cults like the Assemblies of God. I did, however, and got slaughtered. I'm not the only one.

It is difficult to consider Christianity today a legitimate arm of God when these kinds of things take place regularly in the churches. The god of cult Christianity such as the Assemblies of God is a home-wrecking, closet psychopath, lying in wait for his next victim. I cannot accept this church-god as the true God.

The intense hatred that I found myself subjected to by born-again Christians, so vicious that it could only have been spawned by hell itself, affected everyone I tried to minister to, finally climaxing with a tragic consequence.

A tough prostitute gave her heart to Jesus as the result of a talk I had with her on a New York City street. Overjoyed, she went to an Assemblies of God church in Manhattan, the next Sunday. When she told the pastor of her conversion, he was quite interested. Then he asked her how it happened. When she mentioned my name, the man rudely turned his back on her and walked away.

This new child of God, totally crushed, as if God Himself had rejected her, went out and committed suicide. Another prostitute, who had been open to try God, told me what happened, then said: "Thanks a lot for bringing us the 'good news' of Jesus!"

I abandoned all future plans I had for Christian service. For what purpose should I, or anyone else, be a minister? To get trusting people involved with these insensitive hypocrites who would destroy them? I know of at least one young woman who would be alive today had I not introduced her to the "Christian way of life." For this reason alone I would never become involved in it again.

I will never forget the incredible stories, totally unfounded, which the church circulated about me. The born-agains, who knew better, were not only *willing* to believe these sick rumors, they were *anxious* to.

This defect in character is the logical outgrowth of Christian teaching. Christians are taught that "sin" lurks around every corner and in everyone—that there are no exceptions. They *must* look for the worst in everyone, to protect and edify their own souls. The Christian is, in effect, trained to find evil in every situation.

As to the suggestion that I might have a ministry to ministers, this is an intriguing possibility and could do some real good. There are other serious matters I must confront first in my quest for truth, however. I have come to the conclusion that the Bible is *not* the authentic word of God. It has been tampered with by man in order to give man a powerful tool with which to manipulate other people. An exhausting study is being conducted by G. Wayne Taylor in Southern California which will eventually be published in a book. Mr. Taylor has discovered that there are seventeen versions of the King James Bible. Each version was written to manipulate the people of a particular era.

I have learned that the *first* books of the New Testament were written by the Apostle Paul. The Gospel writers came *later*. Matthew, Luke, and John plagiarized the writings of Mark. In closely examining Mark's writings, it has become clear that Mark knew nothing about the customs or traditions of Palestine. This means that he possibly was not even there. Why else would each of these "witnesses" to Christ's crucifixion have a different version of what was written over the head of Jesus, or indeed the last words of Jesus? I think we have all been had.

I will now offer you a shocking truth that man not only tampered with the Bible in order to control his fellow man, but that man did a King (James) screw-up in the process. Before reading on, be sure you are sitting down. You might even want to pour yourself a glass of wine, or possibly a stiffer drink.

One day while randomly reading my Bible, I made a startling discovery. After reading 2 Kings 19, I flipped a number of pages and read some more. To my astonishment, I found myself reading the same words. I turned back to 2 Kings 19. Now class, open your Bibles to 2 Kings 19—and also to Isaiah 37. These books are, word for word, identical! No Bible scholar has been able to give me a satisfactory explanation for this.

Before I would ever reenter the ministry, I would have to re-research the entire Bible and try to learn what God *really* wanted to say, if indeed any part of His word is actually contained there. It sickens me to realize that during the ten years I served in the ministry I was taking part in a lie—the greatest fraud ever perpetrated against man. Like the rest, I fell for it—and for me, at a great cost.

VIII

Potpourri

For we write none other things unto you, than what ye read or acknowledge.

2 Corinthians 1:13

The most startling letter I received in response to *Don't Call Me Brother* came from a relative I didn't know about. According to her letter, I am related to the most famous family in the world, with a name that still sends shudders up my spine every time I hear it.

May 28, 1989

Dear Alvie Lee Keeney, Jr., Maddox,

I have just finished reading your book *Don't Call Me Brother*, and wanted you to know some things about the other side of your family. Enclosed is a copy of the epitaph of your great-great grandmother. Please note the birthplace and maiden name. She is supposedly, according to Irish records, a sister of the mother of Rose Fitzgerald Kennedy. How ironic, if you are a distant cousin of that family.

Your grandmother was Augusta Lulu Franklin Keeney, the daughter of Robert Franklin. James Salvester Keeney, your grandfather, was either ¼ or ½ American Indian. That "Roman" nose of your father's is really an Indian nose and this heritage is probably the cause of your high cheekbones. And the black wavy hair and blue eyes of your father is from the "black Irish" who were descendants of the Spanish whose ship the Armada sank off the coast of Ireland. He was incredibly good looking, but I wouldn't say he was a womanizer.

It has been over TV in recent years that the FBI & CIA have conducted such investigations on private, innocent citizens as you spoke of in your book. How unfortunate that they waste American taxes on such fruitless, destructive missions, and I believe Jane Fonda is an example. These investigations were probably initiated by someone's paranoia that information which these individuals "might" divulge will affect their career or "compromise national security," when, in actuality, most people have all they can handle just minding their own business.

I am also a strong *believer* and I believe our works, and along with everyone else's, are written in the book of life and that judgment will be meted out accordingly. In the end justice is served.

Have you read the passages in the Bible regarding the *daily* proving of spirits to be sure that they are of God, and, if they are not of God, be excluded from your life?

I know we are not aware of all the teachings of the Bible at once. That we grow in knowledge and wisdom and some things are more difficult to absorb than others. Some lessons take years to learn which may be caused by difficulties and deficiencies in our circumstances in early life.

The circumstances of your early life appear to have been very contributory to your vulnerability to the hold this cult had on you. Almost putting you in a position of complete helplessness. Your book indicates that you learned slowly but well the lesson and finally came to the conclusion of what your reality is.

I do *believe* that all is taken care of in time and the wheels of justice grind so slowly, that there is always evil in the hearts of men. That God has the last say. That God's truth proves itself and needs no justification by mortal man. That He takes care of His own in spite of mortal man and will

expose His truth whenever He so desires *regardless* of mortal
man! May God bless you and keep you always!

Your Cousin,

G.C.
Oklahoma

I had to sit down after reading this letter: me, a cousin to the Kennedy
brothers! Maybe this would explain the FBI snooping in my life!
In another letter from my cousin I learned that my father passed
away August 23, 1989. Thanks to the FBI, who succeeded in turning
him against me, my father refused to see me right up to the end.

The government spies still monitor my mail, and periodically
bug my telephone. They pull out and listen to every audio and video
tape sent to me. They don't even bother to rewind the tapes before
sending them on. Some tapes never even reach me. There is a bright
side to all of this. Followers of the late William Branham have sent
me stacks of tapes of his sermons. Perhaps this will explain why
my local area FBI agents are daffier than usual these days.

Lawyer letters are always interesting, but this one was a classic!
I reread it several times and still had a hard time believing that
this law firm could actually be serious, considering the circumstances
of my experience, to attempt to enlist my aid.

The firm of Duplass, Witman & Zwain wanted me to supply
information about Marvin Gorman, who was suing one of its clients,
Allan McDonnel, for libel and slander.

I found this request galling. This man actually solicited my help
in *defending* a member of the Assemblies of God against a minister
that the church destroyed and threw out. It is the only letter I did
not answer. I wanted to wait until now, when I could do so publicly.
The lawyer mistakenly believes that I am just out "to get" evangelists,
and that I would assist his clients in damaging Rev. Gorman's very
justifiable case against them.

Rev. Gorman has freely admitted that he made one indiscretion—an affair—and that is what I referred to on "Geraldo." Rev.
Gorman expressed sincere regret and repentance over that unfortunate situation. I do not believe that he had the other affairs that
the Assemblies of God has charged him with.

All of these false accusations stem from jealousy. I have personally seen it and experienced it from my earliest days in the ministry. Marvin Gorman's dismissal from the Assemblies of God had absolutely nothing to do with his moral character. Led by his neighbor, Jimmy Swaggart, the Assemblies of God wanted him out—period. Marvin Gorman was railroaded.

Rev. Gorman is the victim; he is the one I would help if asked. His complaint is valid. I can verify that the Assemblies of God is not only capable of this, but has a history of playing such dirty tricks. Rev. Gorman and his attorneys are invited to use any and all of this material in their case. If requested, I would be happy to testify in behalf of Rev. Gorman personally.

Somehow my name wound up on a pastors' mailing list and I received an envelope from Virgil W. Hensley, Inc., Publisher, in Tulsa, Oklahoma, the birthing place for many religious phenomena. Over the window with my misspelled name (A MILS) dangled the bait: "You, too, can guide your church to greater financial success this year!" On the left side of the envelope under the sender's name, surrounded by gold shading, were the following quotes: "Our income increased $500 weekly!"—Charles Sandstrom, First Church of God, Iowa. "Had a 16% increase in giving in '87 and 32% in '88!"—Rex Poore, First Presbyterian Church, California. "Had a 50% increase in pledges!"—Father James Gunther, St. Lawrence Catholic Church, California. "First successful stewardship drive in the history of this church!"—Rev. Jack McCann, Congregational Church, Maine.

The brochure-letter that this company enclosed devoted most of the first page to a tease-appeal. One of the five points states: "It Helps You Increase Overall Giving Of Your Members By Motivating Them To Their Fullest Giving Potential." Then the net begins to be drawn:

Dear Pastor:

Are your people giving to their *full* potential in support of the Lord's work through your church?

Would you like for them to? Would you like for them to become more dedicated stewards, committing more of their income to the cause of Christ week after week?

After explaining how their carefully composed appeal letters, etc., have *"helped thousands of churches like yours raise the level of giving* among their members, many reaching *record levels* for the first time in their church's history," their method is detailed:

REACHES *ALL* YOUR MEMBERS [their italics]

When your manual arrives, note that the heart of the campaign is a series of *four warm, sensitive Bible-centered appeal letters* with accompanying brochures, envelopes and commitment form.

The letters let you reach all your members in the privacy of their homes. See the value of this? It means each letter enables you to place a *warm, Bible-centered message of love and commitment* in the hearts of your members. A message that *relates the act of stewardship to the Christian life.* I know of no easier, more effective way to accomplish this.

In addition, the program also includes an assortment of *persuasive* support items such as:
follow-up lettersbulletin inserts***posters***lapel pins***sermons***Sunday School lessons***and thank-you acknowledgments. . . . as well as simple, east-to-follow instructions that take you step-by-step through the campaign. Each one designed to make your stewardship campaign more successful. [All italics mine.]

It is a sad state of affairs that the church of Jesus Christ so lacks sincerity and warmth that it must hire professional outside firms to *create* "warm, Bible-centered messages of love" to mislead the faithful into believing that these canned phrases express a genuine caring spirit on the part of the church. It also proves that this bogus church-love is *only* for the purpose of separating the trusting, lonely, and vulnerable from their money.

Notice how this firm *creates* "A message that *relates the act of stewardship to the Christian life.*" The use of the word "stewardship" has made many preachers wealthy. Steward means trustee. In the church world this has come to mean a trustee of what God has placed in your hands for His work, and the key word and idea is GIVING, to the preacher of course. Notice how the faithful are led to believe that their position with Christ is tied to how much money they give to the preachers, or in classier terms, "the act of stewardship." This is exactly the highly successful fraud practiced by all of the televangelists. This is not only *unscriptural*, but an example of blasphemy. Notice also how they begin teaching this to your children in Sunday Schools to be sure they are indoctrinated by the time they are adults.

In an effort to place them ahead of their competitors, Virgil W. Hensley, Inc., made the following closing statements under the hook "Unmatched Results."

> Other stewardship programs include some of the same things as ours. But none match our campaign in quality and results.
>
> That's because all our stewardship materials are prepared by *professionals* who are *experts in creating, writing and illustrating powerful stewardship appeals.* [Italics mine.]

If the pastor's impulse for greed has not been thoroughly stimulated thus far, an additional page to clench the sale is headed: "15 Reasons Why This Campaign Will Work For You." With a few lines of explanation under each one, they are listed thus: (1) Successful *Technique* (2) Ease of Use (3) Nothing Special Required (4) Uncomplicated (5) Less Work (6) *Controlled Message* (7) Privacy (8) Education [perverting the Scriptures to accomplish the goal] (9) Complete Coverage (10) Changes Yearly (11) Giving Patterns (12) More Income (13) Proven Successful (14) Low Cost [in comparison to the income that is generated by this ploy] (15) Long-Range Benefits.

So successful is this technique, employing as it does every psychological weapon in the book, that Hensley offers a 100% satisfaction guarantee.

At present, Virgil Hensley, Inc., has 30,000 churches hooked into their system, and the number is growing as competing pastors strive to "keep up with the Joneses."

A list of twenty-five respected ministers who have made glowing testimonies regarding the program was appended to the end of the brochure. Their stature was meant to impress—and to encourage me to buy into the program.

Within a month after receiving Hensley's pitch for my bucks in exchange for instructions on how to milk my trusting parishioners to the limit, I received an official-looking letter from the American Christian Leadership Council, Atlanta, informing me that I had been nominated to be honored in the 1989 edition of *Who's Who in American Christian Leadership*. "This distinguished volume will not only recognize well-known Christian leaders, but also many whose quiet but continued effort is of great importance in keeping alive the basic values of the American Christian spirit."

The letter goes on to pump up the invaluable contribution I have made to stress moral and Christian values and to "work against agents who seek to erode our heritage and our liberty." Rick C. Ernst, the Executive Director of the Council, gave me a fifteen-day deadline to furnish him with biographical material for the listing.

Mr. Ernst included attractive pictures and information about the handsome volume in which I would be immortalized, which I could purchase for only $84.95. Also available for purchase was a personalized plaque to commemorate my induction for $64.95, plus an engraved personalized walnut frame wall clock extolling the honor for $106.95. A special package of all three of these items went for $256.85. Mr. Ernst stated, not too convincingly, that no purchase or donation would be required for this recognition.

I sent in the biographical information immediately, fulfilling my deadline requirements. On December 7, 1989, I received another letter from the Executive Director offering me his heartfelt congratulations. The American Christian Leadership Council was delighted to announce that I had been accepted for inclusion in the 1989 publication, *Who's Who in American Christian Leadership*. "Because of you and other people like you, the Spirit of Liberty is alive and secure for future generations to enjoy and cherish."

The letter praised my virtues, including my "commitment of devotion to Christian principles, depth of patriotism, and my faith." Because of me, the American Christian Spirit continues, and on behalf of all those who I have served, the Council thanked me and "to God be the glory." Under the Executive Director's signature, a postscript continued the message: "It is very important we speak with you before our cut-off deadline. Would you please call our inclusion supervisor Ann Williams between Noon–6:00 P.M. E.S.T." The phone number followed.

Ann Williams turned out to be a man. The sales pressure to purchase the merchandise began. "I do not have the funds to make such a purchase," I said. "We won't bill you for 30 days," the pitchman assured me. "I still cannot afford it," I responded. "Then put it on your credit card, don't you have a major credit card we can use? . . . Any card, they'll let you make payments." As the Christian huckster became increasingly irritated, I asked him if I could purchase the book at a later date. He informed me that I could not, that it was only available for purchase at the moment.

The Christian ego is exceptionally marketable. That's why vanity presses and private recording companies gain most of their income from Christians, eager for recognition. This *Who's Who* book is the ideal vehicle. Most of the "inductees" will buy the volume without hesitating. Christians will pay dearly to be acknowledged.

Something especially intrigued me about my "nomination" to this Christian hall of fame—the spelling of my name, "A MILS." Only one other correspondent misspelled my name exactly that way, and with all caps—Virgil W. Hensley, Inc., Publisher. Nothing is more fascinating to observe than Christians joining with fellow Christians to exploit other Christians. And, as Hensley says in his literature, "To God be the glory!"

IX

Group Therapy

Our group therapy begins with a letter of praise-correction-instruction-confession-condemnation *and* some cautionary advice to the author.

Fontana, Calif.
December 26, 1989

Austin Miles
c/o 700 East Amherst St.
Buffalo, New York 14215

Dear Mr. Miles,

I have just finished reading your book (*Don't Call Me Brother*).

It is wonderful and exciting to know that there is someone out there that believes in the literal born-again experience.

It is unfortunate that you didn't depend on the word of God rather than the ministry to control your life.

In the Book of John, it says to remain in the state you were in when you became born again. Since you were married, your first responsibility was to your family. God would never destroy that which is good for himself.

When I became born again, God gave me a word of knowledge. He said that the Bible was to be expected [sic] from cover to cover, not scripture by scripture. If you take any area of life and apply the whole Bible to it, you will see the simplicity of what God intended for mankind.

All the preachers that I have met with the exception of a very few are in sinful conduct or have been, they are never removed from service. Some continue in their activities and the congregation knows it and does nothing because of the board of directors. They are afraid that they might lose their congregation which adds up to money. They justify everything by saying that the battle of the flesh is a daily thing and some are stronger than others.

This is bull-shit. I was brought into a Christian church by a so-called Christian lady. While I received Jesus Christ into my heart, she left the service to go sleep with my husband. At another church, several of the long-term male members of the church hated me because I turned down their advances, so they proceeded to tell me that God had told them that I was an adulteress and that I better change my ways. I in no way was even dating at the time. Then the wives of these men, treated me as an outsider, I guess they were backing up their husbands.

At another church, a lady hit on me because she thought I had a lot of money and she was going to show me things that would make me fall in love with her. Thank God that God has always been the center of my life and I saw all this coming.

At another church, the junior pastor told me that his job was great, $25,000 per year and only one hour to prepare a sermon and two hours to give it. All told, 5 hours per week he felt he gave to the church. Not bad pay.

We are not supposed to judge people, and I don't, but I'll be damned if I will stand by and allow so-called Christian people to get away with their crap.

I too fell for all the so-called truths regarding the various churches. There are some good ones, but the best is yet to come.

I am very interested in beginning a church based on the triune God. God the father, God the son, God the Holy Ghost.

I am an entrepreneur. I have been in business all my life. It wasn't until I became a born-again Christian that my world fell apart, so I understand everything you have gone through.

However, God has chosen you and you should not throw that away. I know that God has called me out, but like everything I need to be a part of a team. Jesus Christ knew that up front, that is why he appointed 12 disciples. As a team, he could succeed.

Think it over, let me know. In spite of every thing, God is the answer. . . .

I have a great testimony, but it would take too long to tell you how God has helped me through my life.

I can be reached any time at area code [her personal phone number].

Hoping to hear from you soon.

Sincerely yours,

Estella T.

P.S.: I in no way am interested in you for anything more than your mind. I am whole and complete in myself thanks to our Lord. My interest is as stated.

How thoughtful of my new Christian friend to anticipate that I might succumb to her charms and possibly hope to gain carnal knowledge of her through this innocent invitation. One can't be too careful.

I have received this disclaimer from *many* Christian women who've made overtures to establish some kind of relationship with me, *including* the young PTL staffer who slipped past the security guards and into my bedroom late one night in the mansion at Heritage Village (see *Don't Call Me Brother*, pages 162–163.)

The next to enroll in our group therapy session signed in as "His bondservant." In six and a half typewritten pages, the heroine of this session described her own experiences while on the PTL staff. She saw most of what I chronicled in *Don't Call Me Brother* and more, describing it in great detail. However, the outcome of her life proved to be loftier than mine. Being a more deeply rooted

Christian, she stood fast in the faith. Full of phrases of Christian love and concern, my new counselor chided me for my un-Christian reaction to my experiences.

Identifying herself as a "free lance writer," she let me know that if I read anything written by her in the future, I should know that she had written it out of love for Jesus. Apparently, she feels compelled to respond to what I had written with her own story. I wrote back to her and encouraged her to do just that. I even offered to help her get a publisher and asked her permission to print her letter of revelation and criticism.

In response to what can only be described as a polite, respectful letter, "His bondservant" unleashed a whirlwind of verbal pummelling at me—it left me reeling. No, she positively would not grant me permission to print her letter. She had written that letter only to me and not to anyone else. And she let everyone in her church to whom she showed the letter know it, by golly!

"His bonservant," who identified herself as a "free-lance writer," and had this identity printed on her stationery, stated that she had no desire to advance her writing career. God, she said, wanted her to write to individuals, and if she reached one person with her prose, her goal had been reached.

With rising righteous indignation over the error of my ways, His bondservant dug in, ready to release another volley of fire. I was sadly mistaken, she sniffed, if I felt that I was aiding God's work in refining the church. I had gone about the entire affair improperly by writing my book. She too had seen corruption, but unlike me, a weaker vessel, she had been led like the Apostle Paul "in a more excellent way."

My long shortcomings, according to her Word, stemmed from my lack of "fruits of the Spirit." Fruit (of the Spirit), she promulgated, is measured only by how much one is conformed to the image of Christ, not by the number of miracles performed, books sold, or people saved. Everything I had done, she burped on piously with a parting shot, was in vain. She signed out, "Sincerely."

I felt exhilarated to hear from someone who truly "is conformed to the image of Christ." I trust that God will continue to give her a sweet spirit.

An interesting sidelight to all of this, the writer of the above letter is heavily involved in Rev. David Wilkerson's Manhattan-based Pentecostal church. Rev. Wilkerson is the fire-and-brimstone preacher who publicly denounced me a few years ago when I was the "chaplain to show business." In wire service stories, Rev. Wilkerson said that all show business people were going to hell along with their chaplain. Brother W. went on to state that Hollywood people are sinners, cannot be saved, and that Hollywood stars should give up their big mansions and fancy cars. At the very same time, he was enthusiastically cooperating with these same sinful Hollywood producers and actors in the filming of his life story, *The Cross and the Switchblade*, that would canonize him.

When his wife became ill with cancer, Brother W. took full advantage of the opportunity. Playing on the sympathy of his supporters, he urged everyone on his mailing list to send a card of "encouragement" to his dear wife, adding, ". . . and tuck in a little gift for her . . . 25 . . . 50 . . . 100 dollars." And they did. Wilkerson managed to hustle enough money to purchase a Broadway theater, which he has turned into a Pentecostal center, a mega-Christian enterprise that pulls in big bucks. There's one born-again every minute!

More voices were heard, during our session, defending the honor of the late William Branham. They came from the United States, Canada, and Australia. They all said the same thing: They had heard that I was going to put out a book "with things about Brother William Branham" in it. The voices cautioned me to check out Brother Branham's life before "a bunch of false things were published about him." Every one of Branham's followers agreed that He was a prophet of God "who only told the people what God showed him."

I invited a speaker from Cleveland, Ohio, to address the group. His testimony might be profitable to the captives.

April 18, 1990

Dear Mr. Miles,

I read your book *Don't Call Me Brother*. When will it be made into a movie?

I am a 32-year-old Wilburite Quaker, and a member of Alcoholics Anonymous. When I was 15 years old I got emotionally screwed up by a religious cult called "The Forever Family." I was already a Christian, and a Boy Scout, and very active in high school drama and art. But the "family" wanted me to abandon all of it—my church, drama, scouts, and my real family—because they were "all of Satan." Nothing

I ever wanted to do with my life was right. Everything had to be for the "family."

At 16 I had already gone through two emotional breakdowns because I was always afraid of judgment and hell fire. So I dropped out, but had no support group to make the transition. I made a 180-degree turn in my life, and spent the next fifteen years drinking and drugging and wasting my life trying to regain that original "born again" feeling of support, belonging, and closeness.

When my parents were killed in a car accident, I had nightmares that I sent them to hell. And my drinking and drugging got worse.

At 30, after losing my savings, my house, wife, car, and job (in that order), I had another breakdown, but this time I tried committing suicide. I was hospitalized for clinical depression and diagnosed as a borderline personality.

After weeks of counseling, medication, and support from my ex-wife's mother, I joined AA, where I gained the God of *my* understanding, through the 12 steps and the four absolutes. God, Christ, St. Paul, and my father were top on my list of resentments. It was not easy getting the anger and hate out of my system that was feeding on me like a parasite *because I left the cult!*

A year later I joined the Wilburites, where I regained the Christ of *my* understanding. I joined the Wilburites because I found their beliefs and practices compatible with how *I* think a Christian should live. No hell-fire-and-damnation preaching. No singing hymn after hymn after hymn. No offering plate passed around. And best of all, no paid clergy or minister! In silence we wait upon God, and in silence we talk to him.

Every human being is my neighbor and every human being is a child of God. The Buddhist, the Atheist, the Moslem, the Jew, all have something important to *teach me.*

You are right, religion is private, but spirituality is more important. I'm not trying to proselytize you; that would be stupid! I only wanted to let you know that you're not alone.

Thank you.

Bob Toothman

I received this reply to my request for his permission to print the letter.

Dear Mr. Miles,

Thank you for your letter. *Yes you may print my letter for your next book.* I hope it, and all the other letters you print, will help all those who have gone through what we have gone through, so that people will know they are not alone.

I shared your book with my sister. She's been involved in a Pentecostal church for the last seven and a half years, and she got involved in the PTL crap. She even has one of those "exclusive" Bibles you mentioned in your book. I think my sister is "beginning to see the light," thanks to your book and some others.

I recently met a most interesting person. I discovered him by accident. He used to play in some well-known 1960s rock groups.

This guy now lives in his car, looking like a 50-year-old hippy, where he reads and studies the Bible *all day!* Except when he makes his $50 a week singing his original apocalyptic, Christian songs in bars.

I like him; he's eccentric to the core. But he is what we in AA call a "negative power of example." He shows me where I could *have* ended up, and where I *could* end up, if I am not careful and on my guard. He has been completely brainwashed by the Christian cult he was involved in, where he was whipped, made to stand in the cold of winter naked, hours without sleep, long days of fasting, prayer, and Bible reading. *Concentration camp Christianity.* Whenever he speaks, every other sentence is a Bible quotation. And the man has been this way sine 1968! One could say the Prophet Jeremiah lives down the street from me, in a car with quotations of Revelation 20:15 plastered all over it.

I saw the NBC movie, "Fall From Grace." They left a hell of a lot out, but what did you think of the actors' portrayals of Jim and Tammy?

Very Truly Yours,

Bob Toothman

I thought the actors were excellent, particularly Bernadette Peters's carbon of Tammy. But, as Mr. Toothman stated, "they left a hell of a lot out." The full inside story of that mess still needs to be filmed.

My day would not have been complete without this communication from a ministerial candidate with a high-heels fetish.

June 27, 1989

Dear "Mr." Miles,

Since the title of your book is *Don't Call Me Brother*, I will honor your request. I, too, have had a bad deal in my contacts with the Assemblies of God, as have you, and feel that if the church ought to clean up its act, a lot is needed to be done for such. May I share with you some of my own experiences?

First, of all, a lot of what I encountered began when I got out of the Air Force, and went off to Central Bible College in Springfield, Missouri. I first went there in the fall of 1973, and thought I was doing something that was pleasing God. Instead, it turned out to be one of the worst years of my life. At first, it started out good. I went with a girl, named Sandy, from Wisconsin, whom I liked very much. We went steady for a couple of months, and then, one day, she up and told me that something (or someone) told her to "be careful." She said, that I was "the first Christian guy she'd gone out with." We never saw each other again after that. (I always had the sneaking suspicion that she was pressured into this.) From that point on, the rest of the year was downhill all the way, as far as blessings and joy. Too, may I say here, my background is Episcopalian, and I was saved before I joined the Air Force in 1969, and later filled with the Holy Spirit. I later left there for a Presbyterian Church in St. Louis that I liked very much. I am still, to this day, good friends with the pastor.

Anyway, one thing that kept happening to me down at CBC was, I was always being pressured to "fit into our mold; do everything our way; be what we say you have to be; do what we say you have to do." It really bothered me that one person had one idea of what sort of mold I had to fit into, another had a second, a third had a third, etc. It seemed to me there was no unity in that outfit, and it greatly disturbed me. One thing I was shocked at was that some people told me it was wrong to desire a wife in marriage! I'm serious; they told me that "you should want to be single, or you can't please the Lord." I never saw any such thing in the Bible. Too, I have always been somewhat of a character. I have what is called an individualistic personality, which, seemingly, does not fit in with their ways of doing things in the AG. Anyway, I soon learned that if you don't "conform" in there, they treat you like crap. One time, I got into it with Cyril McLellan, the director of the Revivaltime Choir, in a class I was in with him. We were talking about going to movies in a movie theater. A girl, whose dad was a preacher in Georgia, said she felt it was o.k. to do so. I spoke in agreement with her and even said "I would go into a theater and buy a ticket with my money, if it was a decent show, and I quite frankly would not care who saw me go in." McLellan said, "Yeah, but wouldn't that offend your brother if he saw you do that?" To which I responded, "No, I don't think so, not if he had the right attitude." With that, McLellan stared at the door of the room for a few moments, and the whole room got so quiet, you could hear a pin drop.

After that point, it seemed this pressure to conform intensified on me, and I slipped into a very severe state of depression. A lot of people at CBC were going around my back, saying I was "crazy," but I knew better. I saw more people in the Presbyterian and Episcopal churches that I felt were true Christians, and even was treated better by many non-Christians in the Air Force than I was treated in CBC. As the year rolled on, it became more and more obvious to me, that I either conform to their way (which to me, is smacking of worldliness) or get out. One night, one person demanded I conform, to which I responded by slamming my fist on the table and said, "If that's the way you feel about it, fine. You're free to feel that way; but just get one thing straight, because I am only going to say this one time. Go on out and find yourself someone else to pick on, because next year, you won't have me around to pick on, anymore!" A few months later, I left for good, and took a civil service job in St. Louis.

Yet, I still wanted to serve God, and began to attend a Full Gospel church. Trouble followed me there. I was single and lonesome, and made no bones about it, I wanted a wife. All I got was either this mandatory celibacy crap, or the old biddies, the "pillars of the church," seemed to tell me they "needed me in their church 'to help fight this devil out of there' and that if I was to ever leave the church, God would destroy me." (It's funny they never fixed me up with any of the girls in that church, especially considering the pastor's one daughter was going with a guy he hated, and he liked me a lot.) Anyway, I ultimately left there when I'd had enough of the scare tactics and unwritten law that said "I was the old biddies' property." Do I think a guy should be able to find a girl for his wife in the church and not have to look elsewhere? *You Better Believe It!*

Shortly after I got out of the Air Force, went to CBC and then started to work for civil service, I would occasionally see PTL on TV. I must admit to you, I always somehow felt there was something phony about PTL, and that is why I seldom ever watched it. I saw you some time ago on "Geraldo," and it kind of made me think "if you conform to their mold, do everything their way, etc., you can just about get away with anything you want including sexual perversion, even homosexuality, which the Bible condemns." (May I also say, I am not a homosexual and have no such tendencies.) I also occasionally went to visit some "Latter Rain churches," in which all kinds of ungodly crap went on.

A few years later, I went to a charismatic fellowship church in town, called New Covenant Fellowship. Again, they started this "fit into our mold, do everything our way, etc." stuff, and it seemed that they were getting into a thing I later heard about called "shepherding." I was not aware of what is was all about at first, but they were engaged in a little game to make someone made over into their image, or, they had the power to turn one "over to the devil." (I'm serious! They actually told someone that!) I later learned from a friend who broke away from that, that it was designed to, #1, make one sell his soul to them, and, #2, set him up for something, which I was proven right on. My suspicions were confirmed, when once I was told, privately by them, to conform to their ways or else they would shun me and deny me access to their meetings. I thought at that time, "who do you jerks think you are, God?" Anyway, they put me in touch with someone who was a counselor out there, and he told me he would not minister to me, until I "met their criteria," then they would minister to me. At that time, I was miserable and lonely, and wanted a wife. And, I wanted things straightened out for me. I thought "where is the love in this group of jerks? You call this love? I sure don't! This is worldliness and in no way is it even Christian!" I finally went one evening to this counselor, and told him, "I will not do another thing you tell me to do, until I first get an iron-clad guarantee, in advance, that if I do what you say, my terms that I want met, *will* be met and met to my total satisfaction." The counselor said, "Well, then, I won't minister to you, you'll have to find someone else!" Then, I said, "Well, now ain't that just too bad!" He then said, "Yes, it's too bad for you!" I wanted so much to punch him in the mouth, but it took everything I had in me to walk away from him and leave the building. (A few years prior, one of those "old biddies" I mentioned earlier had claimed that my Mother, who I had a very bad relationship with, was "going to pay some young girls to come to my apartment and seduce me." When I think about it, all the damn stuck-up snots I saw in the churches I was in, that would have been a good idea, although it never materialized.)

Some time after this, I began visiting the Episcopal church, once again, but still visiting the Full Gospel Business Men's Fellowship circles, here. I had on occasions met some girls from there, but nothing ever came about. But, then, one thing happened to me that once and for all soured me on the idea of being a minister. I was at a convention in north St. Louis. A man was speaking there, who did something that I later learned a lot of people felt was entirely uncalled for. I had stepped out for a rest room stop, and ran into an old girl friend from high school. She spoke of needing prayer, and I prayed for her healing. I later felt, I needed prayer for healing and went forward for such, seeing this man was ministering it. I must admit, I was disturbed by his tactics of slapping people in the stomach, and saying "you're healed." Then, this (excuse the expression) worm-ridden piece of filth approached me, and asked me "what does the Bible say to do when one person slaps you on the cheek?" I responded "turn the other cheek." Then, this filthy piece of worm-ridden filth slapped me on both cheeks, and said, "This is to show you that because I declare to you that you have a hard ministry that nobody wants. It will entail much persecution, trials" and I forgot what else the slime said. That night after the meeting, I had difficulty sleeping, and was rather disturbed that when I wanted to see him after this, he suddenly ducked out of sight. I, a few days later, vowed to God never to serve Him in a ministry again, and even went to the length to ask Him to "take away the call on my life and give it to someone else, smarter and prettier than I am." I admit, I have made up my mind that if I ever hear of him speaking somewhere, I am going to walk up to the platform, and take the mike away from him, and tell the whole gathering there what he did to me, and if he starts that slapping people around, I'm calling the police on that son of a bitch! (Too, I later wrote him a letter in which I plain-out called him a "son of a bitch." I wonder why he never responded.)

Some time after that, though, I did find a girl for a wife. We were married shortly after that, and are still together. We go to a good church, here, but one great big lesson I have learned is to pretty well keep to yourself, if you are in church circles. I do that, and have no plans to change this, until I can see that the church is showing love one to another as Jesus loves us. I am sure that cliques, clans, backstabbing, throat-cutting, etc., are not living up to the Words of Jesus. I must admit, though, one other thing I saw in a lot of churches, is that the Christian girls are more stuck-up than the non-Christian girls, and I've had my fill of it, and quite frankly, it still gets under my skin. I'm not advocating let's turn our churches into big love-ins, but, I think that that is a slap in the face to the church that this snobbery goes on unchecked and nobody raises a finger against it. I'll be honest with you; there was a time that I had a few hired girls come over to spend the evening with me, at a point when my marriage was on shaky ground, and in those girls, I found more acceptance, more affection, more romance, more kindness, more of a willingness to cooperate for the good of each other, than I ever saw in any of the snots I saw in the churches I've been in.

In case you are wondering how I met my wife, I met her through a computer-dating service. It seems to me one should not have to go to that length to find someone, when if the people in the churches would cut the stuck-up act, we'd be more like what Jesus wants. (Too, may I say, some of the hired girls I had were real gems. One of them wanted me to come back to the town she lived in, and soon, another was talking of moving to St. Louis and wanted to see me, and a third even wanted to become my mistress. Where can you get that kind of a deal in most churches? Too, although this may sound a bit silly, a few of them even got up on the table in front of me and tap-danced on the table for me, in high heels, yet!)

I thank you for your time in reading this, and hope I haven't been too much of a bother to you. I would like to hear from you, and hope to do so before too long.

B.K.
St. Louis, Mo.

"Group Therapy" might be the proper way to define born-again Christianity in general. Observe how television ministers and their guests go off on crying jags at the drop of a hat, while spinning tales of constant battles with an unseen enemy. Others blubber their way through tales of woe and persecution, and how they have been "delivered." Appearing to work themselves up to a spiritual orgasm, their co-dependents in the audience cheer them on with applause and shouts of "Praise the Lord." It is all an elaborate support system of the absurd.

Many born-agains reach an advanced level of this acquired mental deficiency, which enables them to go through life with a perpetual smile and a mask of unnatural happiness stitched on their faces. These drop-outs constantly babble Biblical phrases and quote the Bible with every other breath. They can no longer carry on a normal conversation or even behave in a stable manner when outside of their insulated, church-created environment. These sorry creatures have fled the real world along with its responsibilities. By putting themselves in a protective glass bubble, they think they are able to walk with God.

It has been said that one should not feel sorry for people in insane asylums. Many of the inmates have created a fantasy world and are quite happy with the role they have chosen for themselves, even though their behavior may appear bizarre to those who observe it. Mental patients, like born-again Christians, have shut themselves off to the real world. It is the only way they can survive. While mental patients may have reached a plateau of peculiar happiness that satisfies *them*, most of them would be considered a threat to society if turned loose, which is why our legal system keeps them confined—to prevent them from harming others.

Who can forget the Pentecostal psychodrama played out before an amused and amazed world on August 31, 1989, when God's servant Jim Bakker mimicked a massive mental snap? Hunched over, sobbing so violently that his shoulders shook, his face puffed out like a toad's, he whimpered pathetically, "Why are you doing this to me?" as guards led him out to a marshal's car in chains. I thought I had put on some pretty good circuses in my day, but this extravaganza surpassed anything I've ever put together.

Knowing Jim and the Pentecostal mind as well as I do, this media event came as no surprise to me. In fact, I had predicted it publicly two weeks earlier. Several challenged me, including June Preston of United Press International, when I declared that Jim's nervous breakdown was staged.

The events leading up to that morning set it all in place. I knew that the big problem for everyone concerned would be Jim's inability to admit that he ever did anything wrong. When this became a factor, defense attorney George Davis made a desperate bid for a mistrial. I am not convinced that the "collapse" of ex-PTL employee Steve Nelson the day before (on August 30, 1989) was not planned. Jim appeared to be totally unconcerned as Nelson, who had been compelled to give testimony against him, lay sprawled out on the floor. It was only after his attorney signaled him that Jim got out of his chair, went over, knelt down and "prayed" for Nelson. The next day, apparently renewed in health and energy, Nelson said flippantly, "Well, I don't know what happened. I just don't know. I feel fine now." Jim's attorney immediately filed for a mistrial, but it didn't work. In the meantime, Jim began his series of tremors, screaming out that everyone, particularly media reporters, were turning into animals before his eyes. The court was dismissed for the day, and Jim was ordered to report back the next morning.

A little known fact is that Jim's psychiatrist, Dr. Basil Jackson, was not someone just called in. Jackson was a fellow born-again believer and part-time pentecostal preacher who conducted several "camp meetings" at Jim's new church in Orlando, Florida. Dr. Jackson should have advised Jim that his antics weren't helping matters.

The next morning, instead of reporting to the court as ordered, Jim Bakker crawled under his lawyer's couch, curled up in the fetal position, and refused to come out. It was only because Jim did not appear in court on his own, as he had been trusted to do, that the marshals went after him and brought him back in handcuffs.

Still in a fantasy world, Jim was certain that the court would have him sent to a cushy private hospital to "recuperate." To the horror of Jim and Dr. Jackson, Judge Robert Potter, who had seen enough of these histrionics, sent Jim to the Butner Federal Prison Psychiatric Facility, which is considered the toughest and most inhumane in the United States.

Cable Network News called me the moment Jim pulled the breakdown stunt and asked me to dash over the bridge to the San Francisco CNN studio and analyze the situation for their network. Even though it appeared that Jim had suffered a major mental breakdown, I repeated my belief that it had all been faked, and stated, "When Jim sees what it's like in Butner facility, we are going to see a miraculous and *speedy* recovery." In less than a week, with what appeared to have been an instant healing, Jim was back in court in Charlotte. Does this mean that Jim Bakker is sane? Not necessarily. One would have to be pretty nutty to pretend to be crazy, before the whole world.

Meanwhile, in a strange twist of irony, Stephen Mernick, the Canadian developer and Orthodox Jew who intended to purchase Heritage U.S.A., had to withdraw his offer. A clear title to the land could not be obtained. It is legally owned by the Catawba Indians. A suit was filed by them, in 1980, but the story was buried by the media. Apparently, back in 1840, 144,000 acres that rightfully belonged to the Indians were illegally sold. Heritage U.S.A. is located within that acreage. So, it appears that they will have to give it all back to the Indians, which seems to me to be a fitting end to that part of the story.

Here is a Miles-eye view of the news of "The Great Scandal" in a NUTshell.

Sex-pot Jessica Hahn, who proved to be Jim Bakker's undoing, came to us from—BABYLON, New York.

Tammy Faye started a new ministry in the back of a piano store in Orlando, Florida—called GABRIEL'S Piano Store.

A *Jew* could not buy a *Christian* theme park because it belonged to the *Indians*.

Hurricane Hugo, which slammed into the Carolinas, and later the San Francisco earthquake, were declared to be God's judgment on America for putting Jim Bakker on trial. Hurricane Hugo knocked out the power of Heritage U.S.A. and it was decided not to turn it back on. Maybe God's judgment *was* shown.

When the day of judgment was at hand for Jim Bakker, a regular participant in the sideshow outside the courtroom wearing a clerical collar screamed, "Jim Bakker's constitutional rights are being violated! Judge Potter is going to put him in jail where there are no women, just men!" With a mischievous grin, CNN reporter Jeff Levine walked over, squeezed the protesting preacher's shoulder, and said, "Don't worry. He'll adjust."

But, like the man said, "It's not over until the fat lady sings." When Jim Bakker's 45-year sentence was pronounced, Tammy Faye came out to face a battery of microphones and news people, opened her mouth, and bellowed out the hymn, "The Solid Rock." Tammy had gained some weight, and she did sing, so. . . .

X

The Pastors Speak

Go, stand, and speak in the temple to the people all the words
of this life.

Acts 5:20

When unexpected calamity strikes us we suddenly feel alone, torn
out of the mainstream of life and isolated. Bruised and shaken, we
think we are the only one in this world to have undergone such
an experience, to think certain thoughts, have particular dreams and
desires, or to question established authority.

Shadows fall heavily around us accompanied by the disconsolate
intimation that nobody cares, agrees, or even believes our report.
We hesitate to share these feelings and frustrations for fear of
opening ourselves up to criticism and ridicule, launching even more
self doubt. To take a stand in the matter is even more intimidating.
This confusing and grievous time provides fertile ground for depression to prosper and grow—sometimes to alarming heights.

One accomplishment of my work is to have opened a public
forum where victims can realize they are not alone and to effectively speak out against the abuses of the church. Together we can
see that corrective action is taken. Church abuse and meddling af-
fects not only individuals, but society at large, no matter what a
person believes or does not believe.

The most cautious of my correspondents have been the pastors.
I know the feeling. I felt that I was the only minister anywhere
to see the things that I did and to raise the questions that I have.
These letters have liberated me personally, as they suggest that maybe I was not the colossal failure to God and to man as the church

would have me believe.

This first letter is from an Assemblies of God pastor. The handwritten letter on his Assembly of God church stationary came to me from the eastern section of the United States.

October 20, 1989

Dear Austin,

Thank you for telling your story. I just finished reading *Don't Call Me Brother* and found it to be quite believable.

It seems that so often emotionalism and worldly success have caused ethics and integrity to take a "back seat." If your book can serve to help us correct our course, I will certainly be grateful. If that does not happen, you will remain "a voice crying in the wilderness." In that case you will be in good company.

Having been an A/G minister for 18½ years, I have never had very much access to the upper echelon of the denomination. However, in 1983 I did travel to Springfield to obtain endorsement for institutional chaplaincy. I nearly missed that endorsement, because I refused to agree with Tom Zimmerman on a point. I also was disappointed in the treatment I received from Paul Markstrom. Therefore my limited experience has caused me to see some credibility in your account.

I am enclosing an excerpt from *Of God and Men* by A. W. Tozer. Perhaps it will whet your appetite to his writings. I sense a spiritual kinship with Tozer more than any other author I have read. His other books are: *The Pursuit of God, The Root of the Righteous,* and *The Knowledge of the Holy.* Maybe his words can aid you on your spiritual journey.

I will not consume your time by writing further. I just wanted you to know that I am one A/G pastor who does not view you as an enemy.

I trust that your future will be blessed with the real presence of God.

Sincerely,

Pastor W.
Eastern District
The Assemblies of God

As I thumbed through the stack of mail I had just lifted out of my post office box on January 5, 1990, the sender's name on one envelope prompted me to open it right there and read the letter it contained without delay.

73 Pomeroy Street
Cortland, N.Y.
December 20, 1989

Dear Brother Miles:

Please allow me to refresh your memories about my family and myself. I was the Italian pastor of the Assembly of God church in Cortland, N.Y. We were located about 30 miles south of Syracuse.

You were our guest speaker, I believe the 4th of July 1976. You also were a guest in our home. We had a wonderful meeting with you. My wife got healed during your service as you ministered forth the word. She was healed from an allergic reaction to some medicines she had taken as well as from gallbladder attacks. The following day I remember we took you to the Syracuse Airport where you caught a plane to go to Florida. My wife is originally from Germany and I am from Italy, Rome. We both have an accent which I am sure you can remember.

I just got done reading *Don't Call Me Brother*. I enjoyed reading your book. I found it to be funny, interesting and most of all very sincere and truthful! I could relate to many things that you are mentioning, such as the dealings of the headquarters with you, the general Presbytery reaction to certain circumstances, for I myself went through quite an ordeal with them.

Since you had come to our church God gave us a

continuous increase, with many miracles happening. Our church was packed to the maximum. It is sad to say that Brother Bartholomew and others did not like what was happening at our little church. So they decided to really come down on us and make things very hard and difficult. I finally decided to leave the assembly and go independent. I resigned and turned in my credentials to Springfield headquarters. Three months later I received a letter stating that they officially dismissed me! I am sure that this sounds familiar to you.

In 1983 I moved with my family to Santa Cruz, Calif., and joined the Pentecostal Holiness organization. After a short while we found out that this organization came out with a new doctrine. They even went to court for it. Anyhow to make a long story short, after pastoring in Santa Cruz for almost 5 years, they sent us an eviction notice and made us together with our people to move.

As you can see for yourself, I have also been through many troubled waters with the so-called "Pentecostals." I can certainly feel with you and what you went through with the Assemblies of God. As a matter of fact I even recognize some of their wording and actions against you, the way they did dismiss you and the endless meetings around that famous long table at the headquarters in Syracuse. I have been there many times explaining how God was blessing that little church and how the presbyters were receiving it. It is just too bad that you had to face so many problems, but remember, you are not alone in this. I went through many trials with them, and I am convinced that there must be others that went through it too, or may even be going through it right now.

I am presently residing in Cortland again. I have two sons that are married here and have children. Since I returned I opened up a small place and am holding meetings.

I am planning to move to Virginia. I would love to hear from you. You can mail your letter to the above mentioned address. Even if I do move, the mail will be forwarded to my new address.

If you would like to talk with me by phone, you may call me collect at [phone number included]. It would be very nice to hear from you.

In the meantime I am trusting God and am believing the scripture that says in Isa. 6:7—"For all your troubles you shall have double (blessings)."

I wish you a very merry Christmas and a blessed New Year. God bless!

Sincerely in Christ,

Paul Lupi

Reverend Lupi's letter affected me so deeply that I took a long drive in my car, fighting back the tears. It was not necessary for Rev. Lupi to refresh my memory about him and his family. From the moment I met him, Rev. Lupi stood out in my mind as a true minister of God—the epitome of what a pastor should be, in honesty, sincerity, and integrity.

Many times over the years I have reflected fondly on my experience with his family and church. He is the last minister I would ever have imagined the Assemblies of God hierarchy would dismiss and try to destroy. Why? I could almost hear the voice of Jesus crying:

O Jerusalem, Jerusalem, thou that killest the prophets, and stonest them which are sent unto thee, how often would I have gathered thy children together, even as a hen gathereth her chickens under her wings, and ye would not! Behold, your house is left unto you desolate. Matthew 23:37-38

Reverend Lupi's full name and address are printed with his permission.

The sender of the next letter is the father of an Assemblies of God pastor in California.

September 12, 1989

Dear Austin,

I read your book and it's true, that's what happens to real Christians. Now God is no respecter of persons. The miracles of Hebrews-11 will also happen to real Christians today.

The false teachers of the last days will pervert the scripture, that Christians will get rich in material things. We have a devil to fight and he's not going to make it easy for us.

I have been a Christian most all of my 83 years. I always got my needs but not my wants.

I went to Central Bible in early forties. Had a car payment, a mother, wife & one child at that time. I worked 40 hrs. a week for $16.00. I asked my stepbrothers for a little help as I supported their mother but no help came. I asked the (Gospel) Publishing house and school for a part-time job. They told me God's grace is all I needed. I lost my car, went to the junk yard & fixed up an old Chevrolet and left town. Later I was a deacon in a church & was accused of wasting the church money but I was not guilty, and they voted me out. Years later the false accuser hung himself.

I always tried to keep sweet and God fights my battle for me. We sometimes felt like Elijah, that there's no real Christians out there. God told them that there were 8000 who would not bow down to the devil. In Hebrews–12, many will do great works but will lack love, and be lost.

Yours in Christ,

L.F.H.
Kansas City, Mo.

August 9, 1989

To: Prometheus Books
    Buffalo, New York

Greetings:

I am just before finishing my copy of *Don't Call Me Brother*, by Austin Miles. I was myself an Assemblies of God minister (ordained) from 1974 to 1982. I wonder if my name & address could be forwarded to Austin Miles for some correspondence. Before this book was released I had written to another minister who was planning on writing a book about people that have been hurt by the church. Many had responded to this Assembly of God minister's newspaper ads. Most responses were very negative. PTL is like a curse word to a lot of folks in this area. If Austin doesn't want any correspondence, I will understand. I believe he suffered enough, especially from people who should have shown him love.

Yours,

Jimmy Sanders
Bessemer City, N.C.

My response to the writer brought me this letter.

August 24, 1989

Greetings:

I want to say how much I appreciate you corresponding with me. By the way you don't have to call me Reverend, I have given up on titles along with my elastic ego, I prefer "Brother." The reason that I'm writing is that I was corresponding with a Sister, also a former Assembly of God preacher, who was getting ready to write a book and was gathering data when your book was released. She intended to write about people who had been hurt by the church. I also was cost a marriage because of my total obsession with being in the work of the Lord. I had several bad experiences in the Assemblies, especially with jealous pastors, and, preaching in their churches, many feared that I, being a younger man would take their church. I was given opportunity to preach by an older minister (a true man of God) in a small church no one else would preach in. In time I became Pastor, believing I could build this church. It wasn't until I got a brain-storm to start a new Home Mission work in this area that I found out about the politics involved in getting funding. Not having some relative in the upper governing body I did not qualify for Home Mission funds. I spent four hours explaining my vision to the District Superintendent who didn't remember my name, only the fact my tithes were paid up. I offered to quit my job and move my family, work full-time in building this church only to be told that the district could not afford to start a new work. I resigned the church when my marriage fell apart, only to have the next pastor, who came out of a bigger church, to be funded as a Home Mission church. I could go on and on about the dumpings I got from Assemblies of God people, but I'm past that now. Currently, I hold minister's papers with an independent organization that don't try to tell me how to minister.

I am glad that your book is doing so well. I wish you continued success. In closing, I was a faith partner with PTL for several years. I also did some follow-up work as a minister to people who called in requesting to be visited. I had some encounters with Brother Z and Richard Dortch. If you would like, I could share them with you.

Yours,

Jimmy Sanders

In my letter asking for permission to reprint his letter, I asked Brother Sanders to tell the woman Assemblies of God minister to by all means continue with her book. These kinds of books are in no way competitive. The more information out on the subject the better. Here is his reply:

November 20, 1989

Greetings Austin:

I'm glad to hear that your book has done so well. I don't mind you using any of my letter in your material. I don't have any sour grapes toward anyone. I do believe that my experiences with the Assemblies have caused me to mature. My personal experience with Bro. Z was during a special called meeting to remove the Director of Youth in the state of S.C. I feel that too much reverence was given to this man. This director was removed by Brother Z's suggestion.

I remember during the meeting which opened in prayer someone spoke in tongues and Brother Z called them down and told them they were out of order. Also the same year, Brother Z came to Rock Hill, S.C. to a royal reception. The church went so far as to borrow a limousine from the funeral home to pick up Brother Z. Some of the things that happened at First Assembly of God in Rock Hill were enough to write a book about within itself. Pastor Walter Clark is still there and dictates all that happens in His section. Richard Dortch, like C. M. Ward, taught several years our Ministers Institute at Myrtle Beach for three days and nights every year. Bro. Dortch seemed to be one of the smartest individuals I had ever met in the Assemblies. He made quite an impression on me. He taught that a minister's life must be above reproach. Several messages were given of not allowing money to motivate your decision in serving Christ. Br. Dortch at this time was Superintendent in Illinois, was paid $100,000.00 a year salary, left this to go to PTL for more money. I don't want to write a long letter so I'll start closing. I'll send the letter to Sister Ruth Summey that you sent me. In your next book, there are other organizations just as bad for people as the Assemblies that people should know about. The past several years I've been attending different churches that want you to fit their molds. Being in the Bible Belt, there seems to be a little bit to select from snake-handlers to water baptizers by their preachers to speaking in tongues to be saved, to being in a glorified body. Being independent, I've seen people pulling rabbits out of a hat. Look forward to hearing from you.

Yours,

Jimmy

The following letter is from a disillusioned Evangelical Free Church pastor. It was one of the last letters he would write on church stationery before making the final break to freedom.

June 20, 1989

Dear Austin Miles,

I won't call you brother. This church stationery will probably cause you to suspect a holy tirade against your recently published book and T.V. appearances. That will not be the case. I just finished your book, I read it in about 4 hours, straight through. I read a lot, but rarely finish a book in one sitting. The truth is that I have read just about everything Prometheus Books has published. I appreciate their (and your) courage in confronting the evangelical cult. Let me share just a bit of my own story with you.

In 1972 I underwent a radical conversion, not unlike your own. Zealous friends were bent on leading me to the "Lord." Both of my parents were "born again," my father's battle with alcoholism seemed to disappear (in fact, he hasn't had a drink in 18 years; but he is now addicted to fundamentalism, his substitute for alcohol). I was skeptical, but impressed with the glowing change in my parents. I was a long-hair journalism student at a local college, intending to go on to write or get into the field of communications. My conversion changed me into a "Jesus Freak," and I immediately left college to attend a sectarian Bible Institute in Montana. I read and studied 24 hours a day. Life seemed to be so clear. God seemed to be so real. Answers to prayer seemed to be all around me. It was a very happy time, for about one year. The high wore off, but since I was a good speaker and academically excelling, everyone around me stroked me and praised me. The much desired approval and recognition kept me going. I graduated with a degree in Bible in 1977, attaining a 3.85, returned home to Washington state and went into a state of deep depression. In retrospect I see that I had lost my audience and the academic recognition. I got married the next summer to a very beautiful girl. Carlene had been very active in high school and came to Bible College at her parent's request. She was soon subdued and joined the pious mentality, putting her life in this world on hold. When we got married in 1978, we were both happy to be together, but spiritually unhappy. Assuming that our discontent was of the devil, I thought it best to enroll in seminary. So I finished a Master of Divinity at a Baptist seminary in the Northwest, then completed a second Master's degree in Systematic Theology at Trinity Evangelical Divinity School (I know David Larson from your plane trip and conversation).

While in seminary (four years), questions about the evangelical faith kept popping up. Questions about the inerrancy of the Bible, doctrinal issues concerning eternal conscious punishment, the exclusivity of the Christian message of salvation, the natural fallenness of man, etc. I won't recount the many reasons for my questions, but let me say that I discovered that serious, objective academic research is not what evangelical, pentecostal, fundamentalist religion is about. Study is either indoctrination or defense. Academically I left seminary very confused about the Bible, God, Jesus, salvation, and everything I had taken for granted as a young convert.

Let me also just mention that after four years of Bible College and four years of seminary, I saw so much hypocrisy and inconsistency, that my major battle was not with the devil, but with cynicism. Let me share my first experience of enlightenment about what the Christian world was really all about.

I was a brand new zealous Christian. I was literally out on the streets of the local town when I was not studying or praying. I had been told that witnessing to the lost and dying millions was the point of being here on this earth. I had been taught that one had to abandon self and become a fool if necessary to pull the dying out of the flames of eternal hell. So I went to the streets with a handful of tracts and began to rescue the perishing. The idea came to me one day that a street meeting might be a good idea; with music, singing and attention-getting tactics, followed by a rousing gospel message of salvation. I talked with a couple of other young zealots and they agreed. We decided that we would recruit the best singers and preachers on campus. We arranged for a flatbed truck with a piano on the back, some guitar players and singers. I suggested that it was only logical to ask the best preacher on campus, our President Harold

Longenencker, to speak at these meetings. I vividly remember the meeting in his austere office. He sat there, a man of 45, distinguished and dressed in a very expensive 3-piece suit. After I presented our idea, he looked like I had just given him 6 months to live. He fidgeted and made a long list of excuses about his time and duties, etc., etc. I remember leaving that office, naive enough to believe that the world was lost and dying, and the very President was too busy to pull the lost from the fires of Hades. I realize now that he would have been humiliated; a member of the local Kiwanis, a friend of some of the town bankers, and respected in the general social structure of that Montana rural community. There was no way he would be caught dead on the back of a flatbed truck preaching on a street corner.

We approached two other faculty members, both exceptional chapel speakers, but they too had other more pressing duties. My disillusionment began there. The following years brought many, many more. That is why I could so identify with your book. The hypocrisy, evil, and violence was shocking. I was involved in church splits, pastor-hating crusades and other atrocities.

After seminary, we left Chicago to work on my father-in-law's large cattle ranch in western Montana. We spent most of the summer at the family cabin on Flathead Lake, recuperating from four long years of seminary. I barely graduated from the Baptist school because I was not pre-tribulational in my rapture theory! By then, both of us were slipping in our faith; that year we went to an R-rated movie and drank wine at the cabin one night. But we felt appropriately guilty.

After a year of feeding cattle and cutting hay, I decided that my waning faith would improve if I could pastor a church. I was also applying to colleges and seminaries to teach, but most required a doctorate. Eventually I wound up at Pinehurst Community Chapel, in June of 1984. I also became an adjunct faculty member at the local Presbyterian seminary, Western Reformed Seminary. I thought the time in the pastorate and the teaching experience would move me closer to God and satisfy my doubts. Just the opposite has happened. My time of studying, mostly non-approved books, and my horrifying experiences in 5 years of pastoral duties have left me an agnostic. Various church-related experiences contributed to my wife's near nervous breakdown last year. We are both tired of the cult, and desire to live our lives freely and openly.

As of August 1st I am out of the church. I am waiting for Boeing to call with a promised job in Human Resources, but will frame houses or dig ditches if need be. We are holding on by our fingernails. The stress level is high. We have lots of friends and family that think we are heretics (a term certain church people have hung on us in the past). If loving people and letting them be themselves is heretical, I guess we are.

We also have some support outside of the cult; in fact many have been attracted to this church which are sick of religion and religiosity. My approach over the past two years has been very open and liberal, allowing each person to be where he/she is.

I have rambled long enough. In sum, your book was excellent. I laughed, I cried and I was encouraged. There is life after the cult. I am currently working on a manuscript examining the psychology of evangelicalism, and another on my own life pilgrimage.

Don't let the critics get you down. Continue to speak up. There are thousands out there who are literally trapped in the evangelical cult. Jesus originally came to release the captives. Anything which achieves that goal is according to the original spirit of Jesus. [Italics mine.]

I am enclosing a couple of articles you may have already read. Dr. M. Scott Peck has been the most helpful in my recovery from fundamentalism, especially *The Road Less Traveled* and *The Different Drum*. I am enclosing a chapter from *Different Drum* on stages of spiritual growth.

I'm also enclosing a publication I have read and written for, once called *Verdict* but now called *Quest*. These people have been freed from the tyranny of religion and are passing that message along to others.

Again, thank you so much, Mr. Miles, for being there. May rich success and happiness be yours in the years to come.

Sincerely (a brother of sorts),

Mike Bogar
Everett, Wash.

The next letter comes to us from a minister, evangelist, and Bible teacher. His church affiliation is with the United Pentecostal Church International, which has its headquarters in Hazelwood, Missouri. His views and defense of me do not necessarily reflect the opinion of that organization. He is willing to let his personal views be made known along with his name.

November 24, 1989
Los Angeles, Calif.

Dear Austin:

I am a United Pentecostal minister, and have just finished reading your book, *Don't Call Me Brother.* I deeply appreciated it and appreciate you. May I say that I feel very sorry for the things that had happened to you while you were in the ministry. I believe that God was using you to try to bring the Assemblies of God back to where they once were but they rejected it and tried to kill the prophet.

In my mind I went with you through every page into all the places you went and could see the things you went through. I could see the powers working against you and could feel the sting of rejection and I began to pray, and examine my own ways, and I asked God to "please help me."

I began to think about Elijah when he fled from Jezebel, and he came to a cave and lodged there and the word of the Lord came to him and said unto him, "what doest thou here Elijah?" and he said, "I have been very jealous for the Lord God of hosts . . . for the children of Israel have forsaken thy covenant, thrown down thine altars, and slain thy prophets with the sword and even I only am left and they seek my life to take it away. . . ." and the Lord said unto him, "go, return on thy way to the wilderness of Damascus: and when thou comest, anoint Hazael to be king over Syria. . . ." 1 Kings 19:9–15 (KJV). In other words, God was telling Elijah, *"I'm not done with you yet."*

I pray that you and your family will be reunited and that God will heal all the wounds, and please don't give up on all of us, and especially don't give up on God. I will recommend your book to my friends for it has helped me and I will long remember it.

Enclosed is a self-addressed stamped envelope. If you would care to write me I would love to hear from you.

Sincerely,

Robert F. Webb

Pentecostal "Deliverance" churches and ministers are numerous. According to their theology, the cause of all independent human action is demon-orchestrated. The emphasis in these churches is on inherited sin. In their "theology," devils lurk on all sides ready to snatch up the souls of the unwary and cast them into hell. The destiny of all adherents is perpetual participation in a fierce struggle against the powers of darkness in which there is no relief. Life is drudgery—a testing ground to show proof of fitness for heaven. Happiness is not to be expected in this life, in any form. Indeed, anyone who enjoys life is suspected of being under the influence of Satan, with confirmed reservations in hell.

The next letter, from a lay preacher of such a deliverance church, gives an excellent insight into their message and mentality. I originally intended to edit this lengthy letter, but then felt that it would be a disservice to my readers to do so. I have decided to publish the letter unabridged, with all Scripture verses cited, so that everyone can read what these churches are cramming into the minds of their followers—in many cases our kids, who have been recruited on school campuses.

According to mental health professionals I have consulted, a constant diet of this doctrine can induce mental illness. This kind of teaching is prevalent in Assemblies of God and other Pentecostal churches. Small wonder that many devotees become dysfunctional in society and end up in satanic cults. The Pentecostal churches, which devote so much of their message to the power of the devil, are the spawning ground for Satan worship.

Pay close attention to this disclaimer. Those under the age of eighteen should not read the next few pages. WARNING: Constant exposure to the following can cause disorientation, psychotic fear, depression, and dependency.

La Crescenta, Calif.
October 23, 1989

Greetings, Mr. Austin Miles:

I have read your book—*Don't Call Me Brother.* Quite revealing! Your book is an absolute confirmation of what I have discovered myself.

> "There hath no temptation taken you but such as is common to man."

At this time, I would like your undivided attention and I'll make an effort not to use any trite remarks or expressions that might bore you in any way. I'm quite well aware of the fact that nobody ever asked your permission if you would like to be born into this sin cursed world. In fact, if somebody asked me if I wanted to be born into a world full of damnable circumstances and situations that is inevitably to come my way after being born into this world, I would probably have said to them without giving thought to the matter, "HELL NO!"

Most, if not all, would have remained unborn to this day if they knew what was going to befall them after they are born.

> "So I returned, and considered all the oppressions that are done under the sun: and behold the tears of such as were oppressed, and they had no comforter; and on the side of their oppressors there was power; but they had no comforter. Wherefore I praised the dead which are already dead more than the living which are yet alive. Yea, better is he than both they, which hath not yet been, who hath not seen the evil work that is done under the sun."

But, here we are, both you and I, and the whole human race that is alive and breathing today. We are all who are living today, given an absolute definite choice in this life. We can give God the finger with defiance, or we can submit ourselves to God's sovereign will so He can work through yielded obedient vessels. To obey or disobey is a choice that is ever set before us who are still living. And what we choose is going to have an absolute boomerang effect upon each and every one of us.

> "Be not deceived; God is not mocked: For whatsoever a man soweth, that shall he also reap."
> "To them who by patient continuance in well-doing seek for glory and honor and immortality, eternal life: But unto them that are contentious, and do not obey the truth, but obey unrighteousness, indignation and wrath. Tribulation and anguish, upon every soul of man that doeth evil, of the Jew First, and also of the Gentile; But glory, honour, and peace, to every man that worketh good, to the Jew first, and also to the Gentile: For there is no respect of persons with God."

It's obvious, after reading your book—*Don't Call Me Brother*, that you went through some severe knocks after your "born-again" experience. And, yes, it is without question, that you have pinpointedly discovered the most revolting, disgusting, demonic side of "Christians," of which these Christians don't want other Christians to know about their dark ungodly activities, but nevertheless this information about them leaks out in one way or another. Each and every Christian individual, whether he or she recognizes it or not, leaves a dirty nasty filthy trail behind them wherever they go. And it is sad to say, that not one single Christian is exempt from leaving a trail of ungodliness that eventually other Christians will start to take notice of. And you know something?

After my conversion to Christ Jesus, leaving my former father, satan (small "s"), and having the opportunity to serve who is now my heavenly Father, God Almighty, I have noticed some very strange things about other Christians which perplexed me greatly.

It wasn't until after a space of time, that all the missing puzzle pieces came together which explained why Christians behave the way they do. I do not know why Christians are the way they are, with my own practical experience. I know why Christians do the things they do, and I know what they must do in order for them to stop practicing sin.

I minister with a Chiropractor who is a Christian at the Pasadena city jail, more than 80% of those who are arrested and put in jail or backslidden Christians! And most of them were repeaters! But now there are only one or two repeaters, which rarely happens any more because of what God has been able to do through two and sometimes three Christians.

> "Jesus answered them, Verily, verily, I say unto you, Whosoever committeth sin is the servant of sin."
>
> "For of whom a man is overcome, of the same is he brought in bondage. For if after they have escaped the pollutions of the world through the knowledge of the Lord and Saviour Jesus Christ, they are again entangled therein, and overcome, the latter end is worse with them than the beginning. For it had better for them not to have known the way of righteousness, than, after they have known it, to turn from the holy commandment delivered unto them. But it is happened unto them according to the true proverb, The dog is turned to his own vomit again; and the sow was washed to her wallowing in the mire."

I heard one pastor make the following statement some time ago: "Slaves who love their chains shall never be free." And we have slavery right here in America today! Christian slaves to sin.

And whether we care to know about it or not, the devil has a dossier on each and every one of us.

> "My people are destroyed for lack of knowledge."

And because of our ignorance, the devil is taking FULL advantage of it. God is fully going by what his Word says, and that's all! The devil is going by how ignorant God's people are.

"Heaven and earth shall pass away, but my words shall not pass away."

If we put God's word to the test (and I have put his word to the test over and over again and again, and it has not failed), it will come out right every single time! without fail! When I see and read about what so and so had done (and I'm no better off than any other Christian individual, I've failed God a number of times without even trying), it's a constant reminder that we should be observing how God would want each and every one of us to walk.

"See then that ye walk circumspectly, not as fools, but as wise, Redeeming the time, because the days are evil."

I have had hordes of evil spirits cast out of me, out of this flesh that I live in, and there has been a positive change in my life, even those who are out of the way (nonChristians) have noticed an absolute difference about myself. When we take God at his WORD, and act according to what it actually says, a shock of reality manifests the way God's Word says it would! What is happening to this country as a nation and what is happening to Christians in this nation, is a direct result of disobedience to God's written word. This country is already under all ten planks of the communist manifesto, and will soon fully merge with the U.S.S.R.

Many pastors here in America are feeding God's people misinformation about what God's word says, and this is causing "MASS CONFUSION." Here is a list of some of the heresies actually being taught to God's people:

Jesus died spiritually.
Once saved, always saved.
Christians can't have demons.
The Pre-trib., Mid-trib., Post-trib. Heresy.
Etc., etc., etc., etc.

The third in this list is what I want to bring out into the open now. Many of the pastors in this country are teaching error when they say that a Christian cannot have a demon. It's not a question whether or not a Christian can have a demon, but how many demons he or she might have. I've heard many Christians say: "How can the Holy Spirit stay inside the same body filled with demons?" I've also heard from many Christians who say: "Greater is he that is in you than he that is in the world."

The last part of 1 John 4:4 is great! God is a gentle man and will not go against any man's will. If a Christian likes the demons that he or she has, fine! God will let the demons wreak havoc in his or her life. How can the Holy Spirit stay inside the same body filled with demons? Listen, the Holy Spirit is not the least bit scared of a bunch of demons. God saved your spirit, and that's all! When we asked God to save us, by our accepting the Lord Jesus Christ as our personal Saviour, our spirit is what was saved, not our minds, emotions, not our flesh.

God has already done his part, so now it is left up to us to do our part and start cleaning house, God's temple, the Holy Spirit's temple. When God sends the comforter to take up residence in a person's body, that doesn't mean that all demons instantly vanish within a fraction of a second! If that were absolutely true, every Christian around the world would be as clean as a pin and would not do any of the things that are plaguing a multitude of Christians today.

If a Christian who doesn't believe that Christians have any demons at all were asked: "Why do you smoke cigarettes, why do you commit fornication, why do you lie and cheat and steal for?"

Many of them say: "That's the flesh acting up." My question is: "What do you think is motivating your flesh to do those abominable acts of sin?" They normally shut-up after that.

"For the flesh lusteth against the Spirit, and the Spirit against the flesh: and these are contrary the one to the other: so that ye cannot do the things that ye would. Now the works of the flesh are manifest, which are these: Adultery, fornication, uncleanness, lasciviousness, idolatry, witchcraft, hatred, variance, emulations, wrath, strife, sedi-

tions, heresies, envyings, murders, drunkenness, revel-
lings, and such like: of the which I tell you before, as
I have also told you in time past, that they which do such
things shall not inherit the kingdom of God." Galatians
5:17, 19–21

"For we know that the law is spiritual: but I am carnal,
sold under sin. For that which I do I allow not: for what
I would, that do I not: but what I hate, that do I. If then
I do that which I would not, I consent unto the law that
it is good. Now then it is no more I that do it, but sin
that dwelleth in me. For I know that in me (that is, *in
my flesh*) dwelleth me; but how to perform that which is
good I find not. For the good that I would I do not: but
the evil which I would not, that I do. Now if I do that
I would not, it is no more I that do it, but sin that dwelleth
in me. I find then a law, that, when I would do good,
evil is present with me. For I delight in the law of God
after the inward man: But I see another law in my *members*,
warring against the law of my mind, and bringing me
into captivity to the law of sin which is in my *members*.
O wretched man that I am! who shall deliver me from
the body of this death? I thank God through Jesus Christ
our Lord. So then with the mind I myself serve the law
of God; but with the flesh the law of sin."

A multitude of Christians consistently say: "Demons can only oppress Christians but cannot get inside." The following
scriptures refute the above statement made by many Christians today:

"But I fear, lest by any means, as the serpent beguiled
Eve through his subtlety, so your minds should be cor-
rupted from the simplicity that is in Christ. For if he that
cometh preacheth another Jesus, whom we have not
preached, or if ye receive *another spirit*, which ye have not
received, or another gospel, which ye have not accepted,
ye might well bear with Him." (2 Corinthians 11:3, 4)

"And lest I should be exalted above measure through
the abundance of the revelations, there was given to me
a *thorn in the flesh*, the messenger of Satan to buffet me,
lest I be exalted above measure." (2 Corinthians 12:7)

This blatantly false teaching fostered by the theological cemetery or seminary schools across this country, has brought unparalleled confusion amongst Christians. We are ignoring the following scriptures:

"But the anointing which ye have received of him abideth in you, and ye need not that any man teach you: but as the same anointing teacheth you of all things, and is truth, and is no lie, and even as it hath taught you, ye shall abide in him." (1 John 2:27)

"Thus saith the Lord: Cursed be the man that trusteth in man, and maketh flesh his arm, and whose heart departeth from the Lord." (Jeremiah 17:5)

"Let no man deceive you with vain words." (Eph. 5:6)

"Let no man deceive you by any means." (2 Thess. 2:3)

This scripture verse deserves strict attention: "If we say that we have no sin, we deceive ourselves, and the truth is not in us." (1 John 1:8) What is sin? It's the transgression of the law.

"Whosoever committeth sin transgresseth also the law; for sin is the transgression of the law." (1 John 3:4)

In other words, *sin is evil spirits in the human flesh.* Our Heavenly Father is patiently waiting for us to clean up our act.

"Having therefore these promises, dearly beloved, let us cleanse ourselves from all filthiness of the *flesh and spirit,* perfecting holiness in the fear of God." (2 Cor. 7:1)

By now, I've probably said enough in this letter for you to throw the book at me!

But the truth of the matter is, that the LORD JESUS CHRIST had cast out many devils out of those who had them, Christ Jesus our Lord and Savior has given us an example to follow:

"As ye have therefore received Christ Jesus the Lord, so walk ye in him."

As you can well tell, the devil has practically got the Christian churches sewed-up in corruption in this nation alone! The devil has incapacitated the majority of God's people in a horrendous way! Why? Simply because Christians refuse to follow instructions that are listed in the answer book (The Bible). But actually multitudes of Christians are being misled by their pastors who were misled in the "Theological Cemetery Schools" where they picked up their learning.

"But the anointing which ye have received of him abideth in you, and ye need not that any man teach you: but as the same anointing teacheth you of all things, and is truth, and is no lie, and even as it hath taught you, yet shall abide in him."

We live in a battlefield, and in this battlefield the enemy is playing for keeps, but most Christians are too dumb to realize it!

"No man that wareth entangleth himself with the affairs of this life; that he may please him who hath chosen him to be a soldier."

"Be sober, be vigilant; because your adversary the devil, as a roaring lion, walketh about, seeking whom he may devour."

You must admit that Christians all across this country are in a spiritual, pitiful mess. Christians are observing events taking place in this country as well as countries worldwide that conditions are becoming increasingly worse! and Christians are not doing anything to stop communist takeover of the world. Communism and Christianity simply do not mix. Look what happened to the Christians in Russia, they were all slaughtered!

We have so much power at our disposal to transform this world and rid it of all communism, etc., etc., but Christians have been neutralized extensively by doctrines of devils actually being taught in churches today! And they flat don't realize it!

Well, I'm going to bring this letter to a close, but I want

to say that what you did in writing that book—*Don't Call Me Brother*, is a good way of pressing the panic button, and warning other Christians what has transpired over the years in the churches in this country. The devil is more than aware, that if he is going to set up a one-world dictatorship, he has to destroy Christianity from within, by way of having more than one version of the Bible to create confusion and distortion of biblical facts which causes divisions among Christians. Christians are literally being attacked in so many number of ways virtually past finding out!

Please understand, Austin, that I'm not sending you this info. to cause you any upset in any way, I'm just sending this information to inform you of things that you might not be aware of. We all need to be enlightened in one area or another. Hope that I haven't bored you or angered you in any way. Please feel free to make any comments or ask any questions that you might have, and thank you for your undivided attention during this time.

Victor Nyland

La Crescenta, Calif.

The writer of this letter, who subtly suggests that a demon is behind my leaving God's service, is a product of his own teaching and environment. Despite its length and drudgery, this rambling essay should be taken seriously and carefully analyzed by concerned individuals. This letter provides the strongest possible case against school-campus evangelism. The born-again Christians want to teach our children that life is a totally negative experience and put them in bondage by stripping them of their self-esteem.

Critics, who I suspect tumbled out of steepled structures, assailed a recent California Task Force study regarding the effects of self-esteem as "promoting homosexuality and *weakening the fabric of church and family*" [emphasis mine].

Assemblies of God ministers are given this example for preaching against the evils of sin: "If a frog is dropped into a pan of scalding hot water he will jump right out and save himself. But if you put the frog in cool water, then gradually heat it, the frog will not realize what is happening and remain there until he scalds to death."

And so it is with sin, we told our flocks. The devil knows better than to hit you with a big sin right off the bat. You would be too smart to fall for that, so he starts you off with a small sin that you hardly notice as sin, then gradually builds it up to bigger sins until, before you realize what has happened, Satan has snared you completely.

I now see that example in as the Apostle Paul says, "a more excellent way" (1 Corinthians 12:31).

THE FREEDOM WRITER

P.O. Box 589
Great Barrington, MA 01230
(413) 274-3786

June 1, 1989

MEMORANDUM TO: Austin Miles

FROM :   SKIPP PORTEOUS

REGARDING: Your book

Ed Cohen had your book sent to me from Prometheus (Paul Kurtz is on our National Advisory board). At first glance, I thought it would be just beating a dead horse. Once I started *Don't Call Me Brother* I couldn't put it down. It is not only a blockbuster, a powerful tool against pentecostalism, but also a moving, heartwarming story. Ed probably told you about me. I was a pentecostal/charismatic minister for 10 years. Now, my wife and I publish *The Freedom Writer* and our new publication, *Walk Away*. It is my strong hope that we can get together (I avoided the word "fellowship," but that is what I mean) in the next few months. We are halfway between New York and Boston. Please get in touch when you can. I think we'll have lots to talk about.

Sincerely,

Skipp Porteous

I highly recommend the publications mentioned in this letter, especially for those who have been hurt by the church. Mr. Porteous is another minister who learned the shocking truth from behind the pulpit and within the catacombs of fundamentalism.

Rev. Frank E. Ockert, D.D.
Chaplain, Lt. Col. CAP
Post Office Box 98
Wrangell, Alaska 99929

November 7, 1989

Dear Mr. Miles:

Just this morning, about 1:00 o'clock, I finished reading your book *Don't Call Me Brother*. Please notice that I refrained even though we are sort of bastard sons of the same mother: the church!!

I never came close to reaching the place of prominence that you did and, therefore, did not suffer to the same degree, but I did suffer. While I was not affiliated with a pentecostal movement, I was with a denomination listed among the "Holiness Churches." I did experience some similar disappointments. After 16 years in the active ministry I capitulated, surrendered my credentials and united with the American Ministerial Association to retain some "clergy" standing with my Civil Air Patrol activity. Eventually, by the grace of God, I was able to put the hurts and bitterness behind me, coming to the conclusion that "if they can live with it—I can live without it!" For over five years, however, I was associated with a "Christian College" as director of Personnel and Placement. I dealt with each graduating class, of 350 + / - , and know that many of them are now in the mission field or some other place of prominence in that denomination. Even though it has been 14 years since I was "defrocked" (and this sort of news travels fast—I have heard it many times) I have yet to have one former associate, pastor or layman, contact this "back slidden preacher" and say, "I am concerned about you." Not one! So much for Christian compassion.

About a year ago I read Thomas Sugrue's *There Is A River*, a biography of Edgar Cacye, and have read perhaps a dozen more books since on the subject of reincarnation as it relates to Christianity. I am impressed. I cannot say I have come to believe it but I have come to believe that it is possible. The fact that God loves us so much that He keeps sending us back until we get it right is an appealing possibility. Besides, according to the theory, "We reap what we have sown," and, if I have mistreated my fellow man I must come back and be mistreated in the same fashion to learn my lesson. "How do you like them apples??!!"

Sorry, my friend, I really didn't intend to get into a long tirade!

No doubt you will receive many letters about your book. Assuredly some of them will be hate mail, but I trust many of them will thank you for saying things that have been needed to be said for many years.

I am taking the liberty of enclosing a few of my poems. You may read them, or pitch them, but I hope they might be some small blessing to you. "Janitor's Lament" was written as a result of my present employment—a school janitor. The others are pretty much self-explanatory. Without being melodramatic, however, please let me say that I am confident one may still "Meet The Master" along the way and find Him to be all He has promised to be, "a friend that sticketh closer than a brother." I pray your experience will include such a meeting.

Along with my poetry I have included a biographical sketch which will provide you some background information.

Thank you for taking time to read this lengthy letter and please do not be concerned about a reply. I am confident you will have many more important correspondents to which you need to reply.

May God gently hold you in the hollow of His hand.

Sincerely,

Frank E. Ockert

Chaplain Ockert's extraordinary poetry, which seemingly pours from a stream of deep spiritual longing and insight, so moved me that I would be amiss not to include some of it here.

To Meet the Master

One day my path took a sudden turn
And wound down a mountain side
With a babbling brook, and a singing bird,
And a sunbeam as my guide.
Then, rapidly, as I walked the vale
And the sky grew dark and cold,
The lightning flashed and the thunder crashed
And I longed for the days of old.
But as I cowered there neath a sheltering rock
And my heart cried out in prayer,
The rock where I hid became a hallowed place
For I met The Master there.

Another day life was rich and sweet
As my friend and I walked along,
We shared our laughter and happiness
And mingled our hearts in song.
Then it happened! How? I don't quite know
How a friend close by my side
Could lay me low with a verbal blow
And leave me lying with wounded pride.
But as I huddled alone neath a nearby bush
With no one who seemed to care,
The ground where I lay became hallowed ground
For I met The Master there.

Another day and another time
As I served in the work of the Lord,
The people came and the church grew strong
And He blessed as I preached His word.
But the praise of men and the privileged post
Were not meant to be mine to keep
For I lost them both and alone in the night
I would often lie and weep

Then with broken heart and troubled mind
I laid my soul out bare
And my broken heart became a hallowed place
For I met The Master there.

Each day, though different in circumstance,
Brought a lesson much the same
That taught me to serve where ever I could
What ever the troubles that came.
And it taught me to trust my life and my all
To Him who appoints me my place,
Being fully assured where He bids me go
He'll keep, by His matchless grace.
Then again and again as we walked along
I have learned this lesson rare,
Where ever I am is a hallowed place
If I meet The Master there.

Not Me Lord

A ship lay battered by the waves
Where she had run aground,
Somehow she strayed from waters deep
Where ships are usually found;
I stood and gazed upon this wreck
And thought of days gone past
When this proud vessel plied the waves
And braved the stormy blasts.

How could it happen, this shameful end
Of vessel proud and brave;
Ah, better far than ending here,
She'd sunk beneath the wave.
She looked like she'd been soundly made,
Her timbers still looked strong,
Yet here she lay, a hopeless wreck,
And I wondered what went wrong.

It seemed a still small voice then spoke,
A voice I'd learned to know,
That told me ships don't run aground
Where ships are meant to go;
It's only when they stray off course
And sail the shallow strand
That they end up here, as this ship did,
A-bleaching on the sand.

I fell in prayer and cried "Oh Lord,
Oh hear me just once more,
May I not end a worthless hulk
Somewhere along the shore;
Oh keep me where the billows roll,
Where there are souls of men to save,
Till at thy call, still under sail,
I sink beneath the wave."

Chaplain Ockert's poems should be published in book form. He has written more than 200. With permission, I have included his full name and address for the benefit of program chairpersons who may want to contact him.

Just when I thought it was safe to let down my guard and be more friendly to ministers, I received a letter by an Assemblies of God minister named Jerry Scott. Rev. Scott had written Skipp Porteous in response to an article I wrote for Skipp's newsletter, *Walk Away*, which had been published in the Winter 1990 issue. The handwritten letter from Rev. Scott, whom I had never met or even heard of, contained some startling "information" about *me*. The envelope shows that the letter had come from the Calvary Christian Chapel, Assemblies of God, located at 195 North Plain Road in Great Barrington, Massachusetts. Rev. Scott said the *Walk Away* article contained an error. I wasn't dismissed from the church because my "money ran out"—but because I never repented. Repented for what? "Homosexual behavior."

Pastor Jerry Scott did not expect Skipp to send me a copy of his letter. He probably thought that Skipp would simply publish the letter without me knowing in advance. In this way, the damage would be done, and his words would be difficult to retract. This is standard procedure for the Assemblies of God.

Although I had wanted to get a letter like this in my hands for a long time, when I received it I was too angry to call Rev. Scott. I called a close friend, the Rev. John Hayes, an interdenominational clergyman in Holyoke, Massachusetts, not far from Great Barrington. I read the letter to him. Rev. Hayes immediately called Rev. Scott to let him know that he was a friend of mine and demanded to know the basis of the information that he was distributing.

Jolted by the unexpected call, Rev. Scott stammered, "Why I don't know how you got that letter. . . . Why, that was meant *only* to be seen by my friend Skipp Porteous, for his eyes only. It was *never* meant for publication."

"Where did you get such information that Austin Miles is a homosexual?" Rev. Hayes demanded.

"Why I didn't even say that in my letter. I only said, uh, I'm trying to find a copy of that letter in my computer . . . uh . . . I only wrote to Skipp that there may be more factors regarding Mr. Miles's dismissal that should be considered . . . and that's *all* I said. In fact, I will send you a copy of that letter as soon as I find it in my computer. . . .

"How did you hear about that letter?" Rev. Scott continued frantically, realizing the implications of getting caught at something like this.

"From another minister," Rev. Hayes responded with authority.

"I'm going to call Skipp right away and make sure he doesn't print that letter." Rev. Scott continued, "Skipp is a good friend of mine. In fact, I am trying to get him back into the faith. . . . Do you know that Austin Miles doesn't even believe in God? You can see that in his article, and he has absolutely nothing to do with any church." In his eyes, these "facts" relating to my nonbelief justified the lie he was circulating about me. Rev. Hayes didn't buy it.

It was a matter of public record that I had been dismissed from the church for having a previous marriage "that it did not know about." The exact wording of the dismissal notice, dated October 28, 1977, is: "Whereas: Austin Miles gave inaccurate information on his original application for credentials concerning a previous marriage, and at the time of application he was living in a state of matrimony and. . . ."

The reason given for my dismissal was reiterated *11½ years later* in the "Assembly of God MINISTER" newsletter (intended to be see *only* by A/G ministers in good standing) dated April 10, 1989.

In a statement against me and my book, it included the following information: ". . . he was dismissed when it was later discovered that he had misrepresented his marital situation on his credential application in violation of Assemblies of God principles." There were no moral charges against me whatsoever.

It should be noted that the Assemblies of God very much wanted me in their fold because of my money, which they expected to get (and did) and because of my high public profile, which would give them a publicity advantage. While looking over the application for credentials that the New York District of the denomination wanted me to fill out, I asked about the line regarding my marital status, which gave me a choice of married, single, divorced, widowed, or other. "What do I do about this?" I asked Rev. R.D.E. Smith, Executive Secretary of the Assemblies of God, and Rev. Joseph Flower, Superintendent of the New York District. "You know, of course, I had a very bad marriage in my youth."

"Just mark 'married,' " *they both advised.*

"The other is under the blood." That same advice was given to me by Rev. Coleman McDuff, a prominent Assemblies of God evangelist and pastor who had been pushing for my ordination. When they got what they wanted, the Assemblies of God did not want me any more, and used my previous marriage and divorce as an excuse to dismiss me.

Rev. Jerry Scott was more than shaken up by the call from Rev. John Hayes. He had failed to throw the bomb, run, hide, and then watch the damage he had caused without taking any of the responsibility. The bomb had backfired. The next morning (April 19, 1990) at 7:30 A.M. (4:30 A.M. my time), I placed a call to Rev. Scott.

"Reverend Scott? This is Austin Miles calling from San Francisco."

"Why, hello, Austin," responded a frightened voice, trying to feign familiarity.

"I have in my hand a letter that you wrote to Skipp Porteous that states the following. . . ." After reading him the contents of his letter to Skipp, Rev. Scott broke in, "I'm so glad you have that letter, I've been trying to find a copy of it and can't."

"Reverend Scott, I am not aware of *any* charges *ever* brought against me for homosexual behavior. Furthermore, I am not aware of even an *accusation* of such a thing. By what authority are you giving out such information?"

A nervous Jerry Scott, never expecting to be caught and still smarting from the unexpected call from Rev. John Hayes the night before, admitted that he had lied about me. Scott made a conference call to Skipp Porteous and profusely apologized to both of us.

"The devil just got a hold of me," Rev. Scott whimpered. I restrained myself from yelling "bullshit" when I heard him give this tried and proven excuse, used by Christians to disavow personal responsibility for their destructive malicious conduct.

"It's just . . . it's just that . . . we've known each other for a long time, Skipp, and . . . with your stand against the church and what you write . . . well, you just have a way of bringing out the worst in me."

I kept my voice calm. "Rose Marie—she was my wife, in the marriage that you Assemblies of God people managed to destroy— she once said to me that aristocrats are aristocrats no matter where they are, or in whatever company they find themselves. I should think that this would especially hold true for a *minister*, of all people. And by the way, I have never written that I do not believe in God, as you said to Rev. Hayes. I suggest you read the last paragraph of my article again."

I told Skipp that I would send him copies of my dismissal paper and the newsletter restating the charge against me. "Considering how much the Assemblies of God hates me, you can bet if they had anything scandalous against me they would have used it to the hilt."

Rev. Scott started sniveling, "I feel tears getting ready to come down my face. Why, I'm going to be on my face before God when this call is over and ask forgiveness for what I've done."

Rev. Scott agreed to send an official letter of apology for lying about me to Skipp, as well as a public apology to me, my wife Shirley, my stepsons, and my daughter-in-law. He also agreed to preach a sermon the following Sunday, April 22, 1990, about the evil of bearing false witness, with his own confession of having done this to me included. He also agreed to call Rev. Otis Stanley, an official of the New England District office of the Assemblies of God, and tell him what he had done. How ironic. A similar situation with Rev. Otis Stanley is related on pages 295–300 of *Don't Call Me Brother*.

Ministers continue to show their true colors. In Concord, California, a ruckus of several weeks reached a climax on April 20, 1990. It had begun when efforts were made to hold a "Mayor's Prayer Breakfast." Instead of just having evangelical ministers participate, it was decided to invite all the clergy from that city. This created a storm of protest from evangelicals, who said they wanted nothing to do with it. "I don't want to be a part of a unity breakfast," said Pastor Harley Allen of Calvary Temple Assembly of God. "As long as it was a Christian group, I was happy to participate." Other pulpit-pounders expressed similar sentiments. Rev. Dan Kellogg of Concord Church of the Nazarene finally decided to attend. He said he disagreed with the mayor's plan, but would attend anyhow. "This is just one breakfast," Rev. Kellogg pontificated. "There'll be other mayors and other breakfasts and I think there'll be a Christian prayer breakfast in Concord again." Diane Weddington, religion editor of *The Contra Costa Times*, reported on all of this with fascination. The public should begin to ask, "Who are these so-called religious leaders who want to guide us, yet have been unable to agree on one single thing among themselves for over 2000 years?"

The most outrageous example of "mocking God" that I've ever heard of came out of Chicago on April 19, 1990, while I was in the final stages of editing this book. Rev. Erwin Lutzer, pastor of Moody Memorial Church located near Chicago's North Side, banned a little boy with AIDS from attending Sunday School, where "the love of Jesus is taught." Rev. Lutzer has obviously chosen to ignore the words and instructions of the Jesus he claims to represent. In St. Matthew 19:14–15 Jesus said, "Suffer [do not hinder] little children, and forbid them not, to come unto me; for of such is the kingdom of heaven. And he laid his hands on them, and departed." With these words of compassion in the Bible he held in his hand, Rev. Lutzer slammed the door of his Sunday School in the face of a little, dying, innocent, five-year-old child! I suppose if one is in perfect health, with money to give, doesn't ask questions, but just follows instructions, then Rev. Lutzer and his Moody Church (an appropriate name) is just the place to go.

I had met the Rev. Erwin Lutzer on November 17, 1989, in the WGN Radio studios in Chicago, where we debated the subject of Christianity. The host of the program, Milton Rosenberg, had asked me if a person needed to be a Christian or to go to church in order to be a moral person. I had said, "Absolutely not. In fact, I have found the humanists, the atheists, and the agnostics to be far more honest, moral people than any Christians I've met." With a cocked eyebrow, Rev. Lutzer had said, "Ouch! That stung."

I felt bad that I had made such a general statement in the presence of a minister who might possibly be sincere. It bothered me for quite some time. Now that I've learned how hard-hearted Rev. Lutzer is, I no longer need be concerned whether I had hurt the feelings of this bag-of-wind, or any other lug-headed preacher. (Note: After the media reported Lutzer's egregious behavior, he was overwhelmingly rebuked by the public. The boy with AIDS was then allowed to attend Sunday School.)

XI

Sermon to a Congregation of One

A preacher in Michigan read *Don't Call Me Brother*, missed the whole point of the book, and preached an authoritative sermon to straighten out my thinking. Assuming an unsolicited role as my personal spiritual advisor and counselor, he took a special interest in what he supposed to be my sex life and prurient pursuits. Indeed, the "fornication" of *everybody*, especially remarried couples, seems to have brought upon "The Preacher" untold anxiety.

According to my "advisor," my downfall came about as a result of my "ravishing the bosoms of strange women," having been divorced and remarried, and the most serious offense of all, I still loved the circus! According to The Preacher, the circus is an abomination to God—a place for the unsaved, not the saved. "One cannot be a Christian and be in the circus. Good God Almighty! In fact, the actual downfall of Jim Bakker *began* the moment he started putting (gasp) circus acts on a gospel program." The Preacher exhorted me to "come out from among them."

His sermon taught me many other things, with which I would profit withal, including the little known fact that Abraham, Jacob, Isaac, and Noah were great *Christians*, and that it is God's directive that all couples who have been previously married must divorce immediately and go back to their first husbands and wives. The Preacher closed his sermon with a "deliverance" prayer that would cast the "spirit of Ringmaster" out of me so that I could return to God's service.

The most difficult task of this entire book was to go over the taped sermon, line for line, in order to transcribe it accurately. This proved to be so taxing to my nervous system that I had to take a break several times during the preparation of this chapter. What astonished me was that this kind of teaching had seemed perfectly in order and normal to me when I was one of the sheep.

The churches *gradually* build up their recruits to accept their perverted teaching until each mind finally surrenders and embraces it fully. It is the old frog-in-the-hot-water syndrome. Since I made my escape from the church and cleared my mind, I see this demented teaching for what it is, and it's NOT of God.

The Preacher loads us down with endless Scriptures to back up his ramblings. The verses have been set on the following pages so as to separate them from the words of The Preacher. They should *all* be examined, tedious as it is, since these words, cloaked as they are in appealing poetic form, are the same words that through constant repetition eventually enslave the minds and souls of the followers. In the end, the victim is afraid to make any move that might displease God. To ensure that he does not, he is taught he must follow the pastor, teacher, preacher, evangelist, and televangelist, with hell as the consequence if he does not.

This sermon is very similar to the ravings of the "deliverance" preacher in the "Pastors Speak" section of this book. Is this what you want your children to be taught? Is this really what you want to follow? Again, let me be emphatic: What you are about to read is not an isolated nut case, THIS IS TYPICAL EVANGELICAL TEACHING.

I have tried to capture the color of this sermon along with The Preacher's use of words and his stammering without interrupting the flow of his hallucinatory oratory and the points he strives to make. Remember as you read this that The Preacher is doing this to help me! The Preacher periodically pounded his pulpit as he preached and the rustling of pages as he looked up his Scripture passages could be heard throughout the sermon.

Some editing was necessary because of length, repetition, and countless Scripture verses that had nothing to do with the subject matter.

This is Brother Joe J. McKinney, the preacher of Jesus Christ, by the will of God, to Mr. Austin Miles. Grace, peace and the love of God be multiplied unto you. We've come to you, to bring some

things to remembrance, and to *instruct* you about some things that
. . . and discuss with you, some of the things I read in your book.

I read your book . . . bought it and read your book called *Don't
Call Me Brother* . . . uh . . . and there were some things in there
disturbing! To me, and . . . and I'm sure that when they happened
to you, they disturbed you too, when it happen to you . . . very
true . . . uh . . . and uh . . . we just wanta see if we can give you
some kinda comfort in the Scriptures . . . uh . . . y'know we . . .
we . . . it sorrows when we see somebody . . . some of the brethren
fall by the wayside . . . uh . . . when we see Satan steal so much
from us when we have so much . . . uh . . . so we wanta bring some
things out clearly here cause . . . from the way you preach in your
book, there are some things that happened to you . . . and the reasons
you've given for why they happened are the wrong reasons, if we're
going to make up a reasoning from the Scriptures. So we're going
to give you some verses here, and we're gonna give them to you
by books and by chapters and verses, and let you . . . allow you
to go back and dicker with them and . . . maybe . . . you know, ease
some of your pain.

God doesn't like for us to be hurting. He doesn't want you
hurting, and He doesn't want me hurting. God doesn't want any
of us hurting. Why would He send Jesus to hang on the cross and
bear our grief if He wanted us to be hurting? So, and there *is* answers
and they're in the Scriptures. We . . . we have to know where they
are, and then . . . look upon them with the right mind. God is not
responsible for my problems, sin is. And I've done my portion of
sinning, and so have you, according to your book. So let's not hold
God responsible for our downfalls. I will downfall on my own. We
deal with different ministries and different denominations in the
world, and we find so many things going on in there until it, so
to speak, turns us off. But then, we shouldn't let that happen because
God is God, and man is a man. And I don't care what man do,
makes no difference what I do, God is still God. If you see me
preaching the Gospel, at the same time, you know, committing
adultery and layin' up with somebody else's wife . . . uh . . . let not
that turn you off from God, because God is still God! I'm not God!
I say that to make a point, 'cause you're not going to see me preaching
the Gospel, hmmph, and then layin' up with somebody else's wife.
Praise God, no, not for me!

I made up my mind a long time ago, it is Jesus for me! . . . God for Jesus, and for his Scriptures and for his instructions. We're gonna get into it.

Y'know, I don't want to prolong and hold you very long, I don't wanta tie you up. I just want to help you some. And so, the great question . . . y'know . . . we're putting you . . . because in your book, you . . . you talk about how you was, you know, really flying high in the church, and then all of a sudden, the church is the one that brought you down. Well, y'know, there's a question in our mind, from reading the book, and from reading the quotes in there, because I never really heard you clarify throughout the whole book, and that is this: The question is . . . did Jesus call you? Or did the Assemblies of God call you? That's the question . . . that's the question. And you talk about how they took away . . . your wife and they caused you to lose your family. But the Assemblies of God didn't cause you to lose your family.

You lost your family because you didn't follow the word of God in receiving instructions on how to handle your family. Because . . . you probably haven't thought of it this way, God said that you and your wife are one, the Scripture, we won't quote it, God didn't say you and *preaching* are one. So even if God called you to preach . . . if . . . if going on a preaching engagement was going to damage the relationship with you and your wife, you don't go! . . . Don't you think that God's got enough power, y'know, to cause my wife to agree with me going preaching if that's what God called me to do? Because at one point, see, at one point in my life, my home wasn't in order. I mean, me and my wife wasn't in a condition where I was supposed to preach. And I quit preaching for that time, see . . . and that's Scripture. The Scripture says, "For if a man know not how to rule well his own house, then how can he rule over the church of God?" So at the point where I wasn't ruling my house, well, then I had no authority to be preaching to nobody. So I just quit preaching until I retained leadership over my house, and *then*, I went back to preaching . . . though a lot of preachers don't wanta do that because he doesn't wanta lose the money that he will be getting, while he stop preaching.

. . . But my point and throughout these Scriptures, the authority of years . . . who called you? Was it God? Or the Assembly of God church denomination? Because in your book you mention how the people in the Assembly was talking about how you was called and anointed by God, but I don't remember *you* mentioning, and pointing out and confessing . . . that God called you to anoint you for preaching . . . see . . . that's what I was looking for throughout the book. If it's in there, then I overlooked it. If it's in there, I don't remember reading it. But I remember *you* came straight out and confessing that, yes, God called me to preach, and God anointed *me* to preach, therefore I'm going and preach the Gospel. But still, if your wife don't understand, then you should have taken time to make sure that you . . . course you have to make your home in order before you go preach anywhere else.

You have to preach . . . see . . . there are two people you have to preach to first, before you can preach to anybody else, and that's you and your wife . . . you and your family . . . I'll put it that way, you and your family. You got to preach the word to you-all first, and *then* you preach it to . . . to the world. Alright.

The first Scripture we're going to cover, now I'm not telling you how to preach, but I'm doing it because I saw you on a program . . . a talk show. I also read your book, and I could see the pain in your running, and . . . and in trying to be free of the pain you're running in the wrong direction. See . . . uh . . . the uh . . . the circus is NOT the place to run to when you're trying to get rid of pain. Jesus is the one to run to, and you can't be operating the circus and then be with Jesus at the same time, matter of fact, from your . . . your good friend that you listed in your book . . . and you talked about how he was trying to get you to come to Christ before you came, and you talking about how great a man you thought he was in Christ, and then after, you learned that he was out there in California doing all these things here. Well, you see that's what I'm talking about. That's the very point I'm making. Here he is, trying to be and making out to be a good Christian, and working for the circus! In the area he's working in, how can you do that? *When the circus is an abomination before God!* You see you got magician acts, you got all these illusions, you got all these different acts in here, some of them are delusion acts, in that they delude people . . . uh . . . you got the magician acts, see, this is an abomination before God! See, we know that. We know that magician acts and soothsayers, and . . . and . . . uh . . . all these different . . . uh . . . acts of . . . uh . . . delusion, and fooling people, these things are not of God! Alright. So, you can't serve God, and the devil! So if you want God, you're going to have to leave the circus alone, see?

What the problem is, your heart never really left the circus.

And that's where your problem came. See? If you would give your heart whole-hearted to God, then you would have been more dedicated to pleasing your wife. Because the Bible, God's word, teaches you to be dedicated to your wife, and your wife, dedicated to you. That's the first order of business in the priest's life, husbands pleasing his wife, and wives pleasing the husbands. That's the first order of business, see? You gotta do that before you can please God, and you hear 'em all say: "I just want to please God," and they living in a manner that causes the husband or wife to be hurt.

. . . The reason I'm sending you this message is because *God has instructed me to do so.*

You . . . you seem to know the Scripture word, because you quoted Scriptures very well in your book. So the Scriptures I'm giving you I want you to listen to. I want you to listen to because . . . not because of me you see . . . I'm a little preacher that you don't know anything about in Detroit, Michigan. I'm not one of the famous preachers like you . . . like Jimmy Swaggart . . . like Jim Bakker, I'm not like that. I just . . . I am a small preacher as to the world. But I am big in Christ. And that's where it counts at . . . alright . . . uh . . . so I'm giving it to you. This is the word of God I'm giving you. So if you refuse to listen, then this is between you and God. I'm just doing what the God asked me to do. . . . Here I saw you on the television. If you still feel in the same condition that you was in on the television, you're not saved, because you was claiming, according to your conversation, you were blaming the Assembly of God and *God* for the failure of your family. Now God's not responsible for the failing of your family, YOU are. You are. YOU'RE responsible for your actions. Alright . . . because what happened with the Assembly of God was this . . . see, both of you, and you feel that, and also from observing your conversation, you feel that the Assemblies of God used YOU. Well, you all used one another. To be honest and tell you the truth, let's get your thinking straight so you can come back to God. And you might even be able to do *greater* works than you did before. I don't know. That's between you and God. But let's go through a spiritual healing process here. First of all you have to know where your mistakes are, and know what happened, really happened. What really happened was the Assembly of God used you, and you used the Assembly of God. I'll explain it to you how it went. After reading your book here, I can see clearly what happened. You see, you was a man of fame

of the world, that knew how to drew . . . ah . . . draw a crowd.
You drew crowds. So the Assembly of God, they were eager to
grab you as a preacher.

I mean you were there in the headlines . . . years of ringmaster
with the circus—turned preacher. So you got crowds already, see?
You got crowds just pulling in to the church, not because they were
saved . . . curiosity! But they're bringing the money with them, see,
so the Assembly of God used you to draw crowds, knowing that
some of your circus people would be following you . . . more money
for the Assembly of God. But you see, it wasn't one-sided by the
Assembly of God use you . . . you *also* used the Assembly of God
organization, and I'll explain to you how that happen.

You see, if you had started as a preacher on your own, I mean
without any places already prepared for you to go into, you would've
had to build yourself, build your ministry. And you might not ever
have got to be as popular and as famous as the Assembly of God
organization is big. But when you came into the ministry, you came
in riding on the fame, and on the popularity, and in the power
of the Assembly of God organization which put you at the top the
moment that you walked into the ministry. So you walked into
the ministry on the top. You got it??? Because you walked in, walking
on the platform, on the red carpet of the Assembly of God denomination. So you all used one another. They used you to draw
crowds, you used them to advance your popularity and your fame
in the ministry. And if you will look at it like that, see, they don't
owe you anything, and you don't owe them anything. They didn't
take your wife. If you'd listened to your wife, according to the book,
you wouldn't have lost your wife, You lost your wife because first
of all you had too many secrets. And when your wife found out
some of them secrets there you had, that concern your past life,
and all that stuff there . . . y'see what God said about secrets? There's
nothing done in secret that will not be revealed. There's the word
of God again. So . . . Assembly of God didn't cause you to lose your
wife. You did by not following God's instructions. Alright. For God
says He'll call you, but the Bible says to wait on your calling. Well,
instead of waiting on your calling, and get yourself ready and go
when God says "go," hey, the Assembly of God say "this man is
ready, this is a powerful man," Assemblies of God organization says,
"This a powerful man," and people were bragging on you and telling
how anointed you were, and you went on. That's what I meant.

And you came in, flying high, on the fame and the popularity and in the power of the Assembly of God. You used them, they used you. Alright. Here's a few Scriptures I'm gonna give you right quick. Want you to take time and read these, because you need to get back to God.

You do influence a lot of lives. Can you imagine how many people you could actually, *really,* I mean if you *really* get right with God, how many people you could *really* influence? To live for Christ? Because you got a lot of people know you. You're a famous man. And . . . uh . . . I put it to you this way. God tells me, send you this tape. Sometimes when God tell me send people tapes, sermons and messages, you know, sometimes people be so big until, you know, I . . . I be kinda leary about sending it. And then, because I wonder, you know, I be honest. When God first moved me to send Jim Bakker a tape, years ago, and tell him about what he was doing, he was doing some of the same things . . . flying high, and pride, and got away from the word of God. And having *circus acts* on a (gasp) Gospel show?? On a Gospel program?? This is an abomination before God! So I . . . the Lord asked me to tell Jim Bakker that if Jim Bakker didn't return back to God, that He was going to move Jim Bakker and put somebody else there. And I told Jim Bakker, and he wouldn't listen to me and he tried to make fun of me on the TV. He didn't call my name, but I know he was talking about me because he was taking abstracts from the tape that I had sent him, and he was using them and pointing his finger at the screen at me and all this. Well it didn't . . . it didn't bother me. But . . . but I was afraid to send it to him at first, because the man was so powerful. I mean, I'm looking at little me? Send this big man, you know, a tape telling him to return to God? I mean, then, when I realize . . . I mean this man was big in the sight of men, but not in the sight of God. I am and was bigger in the sight of God, but not in the sight of men. And God's the one that counts (laughs). God's the one that counts. So I also warned Jim. I also warned Jimmy Swaggart that there were two things he was doing in particular I told him about, on a recording, and I asked him, to please stop, for I could see that the devil was warning him, and I told him, I said: If you keep doing these things here that you're doing . . . those things will open you up so that the devil can come in and cause you to do something that the world WILL destroy you about. And that's exactly what happened, because he admitted he listened to me when I first sent the tape, but then, after a while, he went right back to doing the same old thing. And it was the word of God that he was disobeying, not me, because I'm just a messenger. I am not the word, Jesus is the word, and I'm the messages, and one of the messengers. I am not the word. When I give, I'm not giving me, I'm nobody but a messenger. For the Scripture saith that we are only servants. One of us plants, one waters, God take care of the increase. Holy Righteous God! . . .

Alright, reading your book there great things were happening, miracles were happening, and because miracles and things like that there was happening around, you know, centered around you, people influenced you, and influenced you that you were really called by God to preach the Gospel, and that you were really anointed and ready. Alright. I just wanta give you some Scriptures so you can think about it, think about them so you can really start laying the blame where it really lies, so you can get your life straight. You will not be able to get your life in order, as long as you're blaming somebody else for your faults. You have to take responsibility. God didn't say you come before Him confessing the Assembly of God's faults, or your wife's faults, or God's fault . . . which God have no faults. God says you come before him confessing your OWN faults and THEN you can get forgiveness, NOT confessing somebody else's faults. So forget about the Assembly of God and their faults and what they did. According to your book, you had plenty of your own. Alright. . . .

God hands out the gifts to whomever He chooses to. The thing about it is, just because God has given me the gift of healing, gift of miracle, whatever gift and I'm operating in it . . . it doesn't mean that I am right. And it doesn't mean that you living right . . . and this is something that I've wrestled with for a long time because I couldn't understand how is it that if a man has the gift of healing, he was praying and people was getting healed . . . uh . . . he was praying and people eyes were coming open and seeing and . . . and he still was not right . . . but then . . . oftentimes God pass gifts to men and men don't live right. So then, the devil in turn, take over and start working, using the gift, but, the gift's of God, but, the power of the devil is operating that gift, by the power of the devil, because the devil is ever-present . . . and . . . see . . . the devil always wanta take whatever God give or whatever God create. The devil wanta take it and create a counterfeit. Alright? You can get the same things almost done, just almost all the time.

We read over in the Book of Genesis there, where . . . uh . . . Moses went down in Egypt after he left Midian, and returned back into Egypt to bring the true of Israel out of Egypt. We notice the miracles that God caused Paul to wo . . . I mean cause . . . uh . . . uh . . . not Paul . . . uh . . . MOSES to work down in the land of Egypt. The soothsayers and the magicians and all offer them . . . uh . . . you know . . . them doodle people around . . . uh . . . around Pharaoh, they be all of them except 'bout two. But when Moses laid his rod down and became a serpent, the magicians laid theirs down to become a serpent. The difference is . . . *God's rod ate up the others!* But they still did it. So just because a miracle is being worked, it doesn't mean that it is God. Just because you see signs and wonders there, it doesn't mean that it is God. Matter of fact, I'm gonna read a Scripture here, in the Book of Matthew tells us plainly. This is what really set me free. This particular verse here . . . in this . . . uh . . . seventh chapter of Matthew . . . uh . . . begin at twenty-first verse. It says:

> Not everyone that saith unto me, Lord, Lord, shall enter into the kingdom of heaven; but he that doeth the will of my Father which is in heaven. Many will say to me in that day: Lord, Lord, have we not prophesied in thy name?

Hey, we're talking about people that actually prophesied . . . gifts of prophecy operating, in the name of Jesus.

> And in thy name has cast out devils?

They did that, see . . .

> And in thy name have done many wondrous works?

And in that line, they did all of that.

> And then will I profess unto them; I never knew you; depart from me, ye that work iniquity.

The works were of iniquity because it wasn't of God's spirit. It was of the spirit of the devil, let nobody fool you. The Scripture has said this, that Satan, in the last days, how Satan come fooling people . . . raining down fire from heaven, and working . . . the Bible call it "Lying Wonders." The reason is, he's working wonders but they're lying wonders because they're works of the devil, and the devil is a liar! So those are lying wonders. They're the same thing . . . some of the same miracles that God works. God can rain down fire from heaven for Elijah, alright? So the devil going to rain down fire. God always said it was gonna happen. He said the devil will come doing that, but it gonna be by lying wonders. Because it of the liar, the devil. Alright. So don't fool yourself. God hands out the gifts, but the devil will also take those gifts if you don't walk with Christ, and have them . . . have you using those gifts for him. Alright.

Now, let's go to Ephesians, fourth chapter, first through the twelfth verses. Get this in mind. I . . . I'm giving you something that I learned the hard way, because around me there weren't many preachers really loving God around me to help me out. I wish it had been. I went even looking for some when I came into the ministry to help me because I was seeking help and wanted help from my fellow man. But it wasn't that many doing it when I want the Scripture of the word of God. I would get excuses like, well, you know, this is the twentieth century now, and blah, blah, blah, you know, when God's word is saying, "Yesterday, today and forever."

He doesn't change. God is the same, see. God doesn't change. A thousand years from now, God's the same as he was a thousand years ago. Alright. Ephesians fourth chapter, first verse:

I, therefore, the prisoner of the Lord, beseech you that ye walk worthy of the vocation wherewith ye are called.

Alright, God called you? Walk then worthily in obedience to the word, in all respect, see.

With all lowliness and meekness, with long-suffering, forbearing one another in love.

Right?

Endeavoring to keep the unity of the spirit in the bond of peace. There is one body, and one spirit, even as ye are called in one hope of your calling. One Lord, one faith, one baptism. One God and Father of all, who is above all, and through all, and in you all; but unto every one of us is given grace according to the measure of the gift of Christ.

Alright.

Wherefore he saith, when he ascended up on high, he led captivity captive and gave gifts unto men. Now that he ascended, what is it but that he also descended first into the lower parts of the earth? He that descended is the same also that ascended up far above all heavens, that he might fill all things. And he gave some apostles; and some prophets; and some evangelists; and some pastors and teachers: For the perfecting of the saints, for the working of the ministry, for the edifying of the body of Christ, till we all come in the unity of the faith, and of the knowledge of the Son of God; unto a perfect man, unto the measure of the stature of the fullness of Christ.

Getting back, it's just another verse about the gifts. Alright? You think God called you to preach? If you think that, or if you know that, then get to it! *But you can't do it,* and please God, and in the meantime *serving as a ringmaster of a circus!* Good God Almighty!! God does not have that! Alright. Four Scriptures we gonna give you. First Corinthians, seventh chapter and twentieth verse. Just to your remindance . . . don't get angry with me. When I give it to you, I'm trying to help you . . . for I actually hate to see the devil take people away that God is working with and has used. I hate to see that kinda thing. The devil do it and I really hate to see it, because God does not want to lose anybody. God wants all saved . . . Scripture . . . it's noted in the Scriptures, God wants that none will be lost, but all be saved. So I . . . I hate to see this done, and it's happening. Remember the Scripture? In second Thessalonians, seventh chapter, where the Lord, about people talking about his coming, and how some will be fooling people, and how people worry and said:

Let no man trouble you about my . . . about my letter, about worry, about my coming.

He said: For the Lord shall come warning of great things and there shall be a falling away, alright? Well, this is what's happening.

This is what happened to you, and . . . and . . . and we don't want that. Whenever that happen, the devil just won in your life. He hath won! He's lost overall, but he won as far as *your* life is concerned. We don't want that. Seventh chapter, first Corinthians, beginning with the twentieth verse read like this:

Let every man abide in the same calling wherein he was called.

Now God didn't call you to be . . . a . . . RINGMASTER! We know better than that. We know better than that. God called *nobody* to be a circus leader! God didn't call you to be no ringmaster. Alright?

God called you to preach? Get to it. If you just . . . I mean if you . . . you might preach in a small church somewhere. Get to it! You might not be able to preach in the large congregations that the Assembly of God has lined up for you when you was with them. But what matters . . . please God. God called you to preach? Get back to it. Leave the ringmaster's job alone. That's a job *unsaved* do . . . that kind of thing . . . NOT *Christians!* And especially not a preacher! Alright. Next Scripture. Romans, eleventh chapter, twenty-ninth verse. We just give you Scripture here and there to just freshen your mind. Eleventh chapter, twenty-ninth verse, reads like this:

For the gifts and calling of God are without repentance.

Now this . . . it is a verse of Scripture to give you for some understanding here . . . that . . . just because I possess a gift doesn't mean that I am a righteous man . . . hmmmph! I used to think that, too. The Scripture comes out to meaning, God didn't give gifts because you had repented of your sin, or was living clean. . . . Often times that person wasn't even born again yet. Y'know, when God gave me the gift of healing, I wasn't even born again yet. (Laughs.) I mean, I wasn't even born again yet! I didn't even know what it meant! It's later that I realized what it meant. Amen. After I received preaching . . . uh . . . which I ran from for years . . . then I learned what God had gave me, at the hour that he gave it to me, and showed it to me. So . . . the gifts of God and the calling of God are without repentance y'know. Y'know God is calling us, and He hands out these gifts, and that's when you find a lot of people operating in the gifts, and healing, and miracles and . . . uh . . . uh . . . gifts of tongues and whatever, and they're not saved people!

Because if God was only giving his gifts to people that are saved, hey, you wouldn't have the gift operating in many places . . . alright. And of course if that's the case, then when they're not saved, anymore, He takes it back. But He doesn't take it back . . . a man who's anointed with the gifts for healing, he retains it, and he can still pray for people and they get healed. If he's not living right, then he'll mess around and the devil will take his gift and use it. Just like the tongue. The tongue can bless God. Hmmm. And I mean *really* bless God. But the devil can also take your tongue, if you allow him to, and curse God. That's what I mean . . . alright. Lets look at another Scripture here, Ephesians four and . . . uh . . . the fourteenth verse, and reads like this:

> That we henceforth be no more children, tossed to and fro, and carried about with every wind of doctrine by the sleight of men, and cunning craftiness, whereby they lie in wait to deceive; but speaking in truth in love, may grow up into him all things which is the head, even Christ.

What you allowed to happen in your ministry, you allowed yourself to be tossed to and fro, by different doctrines. Cause even in the Assembly of God operation, from church to church, you found the doctrine was different, according to your book. Some of them had different doctrines from church to church and they were all Assembly of God denomination. You also allowed the devil to toss your marriage back to and fro, because, see, if you had been operating, according to the word, and make sure and took your wife with you on occasions, and if she couldn't go at the time, then you can rearrange this thing, and say I can't come, and rescheduling, because there was no way, that . . . that the Assembly of God organization could'a ruined your marriage by saying you had womens here and womens there, if your wife had been with you. One thing about it, nobody can lie to your wife and say that you was with a woman IF she was there! . . . God is able to preserve me and my family, and he'll do that if I'm walking in his will. But if I'm not walking in the will of God, then that means I'm giving the devil place, and the devil can come in and destroy.

What St. John 10 and 10 say:

> The thief cometh not, but for to steal, and to kill, and to destroy.

For the Lord saith I am the good shepherd, see, and my sheep know my voice. No other voice will they listen to, so that's so. What I'm saying is, Assembly of God didn't destroy your marriage, God didn't destroy your marriage. You did by not following God's instructions, not getting completely away from the *circus*, giving up that *ringmaster* and letting Jesus be YOUR master, see? In other words, instead of you . . . that's the whole idea here . . . instead of you wearing the title of a *master*, you should wear the title of being a *servant* to THE master, which is Jesus. Amen . . . Amen. Alright.

So we gonna look at another Scripture here, Romans 8 . . . uh . . . these Scriptures just lets us know where we are, what we need to do to get it all together, now I . . . I'm gonna tell you, a *circus* is carnal minded. A circus is a carnal thing, carnal thing, carnal thing—fleshy thing! There is nothing . . . uh . . . uh . . . holy about a circus! There is nothing . . . uh . . . sanctified about a circus. There's nothing righteous about a circus. Alright. Eighth, starting with the first verse:

> There is therefore now no condemnation to them which are in Christ Jesus, who walk not after the flesh, but after the spirit. For the law of the spirit of life in Christ Jesus hath made me free from the law of sin and death. For what the law could not do in that it was weak through the flesh, God sending his own Son in the likeness of sinful flesh, and for sin condemn sin in the flesh, that the righteousness of the law might be fulfilled in us who walk not after the flesh, but after the spirit. For they that are after the flesh, do mind things of the flesh, but they that are after the spirit the things of the spirit. For to be carnal minded is death, but to be spiritually minded is life and peace.

See what I'm talking about? You were still carnal minded. That's why you was in such an uproar within yourself. And that's why it was such an uproar in your family.

> Because the carnal mind is emnity against God; for it is not subject to the law of God, neither indeed can be. So then that they that are in the flesh cannot please God.

So that's what happened to you . . . which has happened to a lot of us. It is simple. Just turn the flesh loose and latch on to Jesus. Alright, that's all you gotta do, turn the flesh loose and latch on to the Lord. Matthew 6 and 24, now this is very important, and you know this but I'm going to remind you. You can't serve two masters, Matthew 6 and 24. Sixth chapter and twenty-fourth verse tells you that. You can't fool God. I can't, you can't. And God is not gonna put up with us trying to fool him and use him . . . alright. Now I'm going to Matthew 6 and 24:4 and I'm going to read it. Now you know the verse but I'm gonna try to explain something to you concerning this verse. There's a meaning in there that the Lord revealed to me . . . one day that . . . when the Lord revealed it to me . . . it's . . . it's just so much more in that verse that I hadn't seen. Matthew 2–24 says:

> No man can serve two masters, for either he will hate the one, and love the other, or else he will hold to the one, and despise the other. Ye cannot serve God and mammon.

Not under the devil here. Now when I read that verse there's something I didn't see, but God brought that out so plain to me one day because I just keep reading these Scriptures, see, and trusting God. It wasn't a different meaning I got, but a deeper meaning to the true meaning already there. What God is saying here is you can't serve two masters, and if you try to serve two masters, what you're gonna do, you're gonna hate the one in it, if you try to serve God and the devil, you're going to end up really hating the one. Now the one is God, and the other is always the devil. See, God is THE one, and the devil is the OTHER. There's not but two spirits out there, the Holy Spirit of God, and the evil spirit of Satan. So there's only two out there, so it's either one, or the other. So if I try serving both God and the devil, I'm going to end up, the results is, I'm hating the ONE which is God, and the Bible says, loving the OTHER which is Satan. But on the other hand, if I choose to *serve* the ONE master, Jesus Christ the Righteous, the Son of God, the redeemer my high title . . . that's not me (laughs) my strong defense. If I chose to serve Him, and Him alone, this is the results: I will hold to the one and despise the other and . . . and . . . and that Scripture's in line with another Scripture that says: I want you to love that which is good, and . . . and hate that which is evil. Give God the Glory!

Alright. I just wanted to bring that meaning out there for you, and I believe that it brings some joy to you. Okay. Now we're going to another Scripture, First Corinthians, seventh chapter, begins the first verse, because this is going to talk about some things what happened with your wife here, because I sure want you to get a healing on that . . . concerning your wife. From reading the book there, really got to you . . . uh . . . and it shoulda. So God wants you to be able to regroup and walk with the Lord. Okay. And . . . and please . . . don't . . . make sure you fight that flesh . . . and don't let that flesh cause you to . . . to hold God responsible for anything that happened in your life. God has set the table for your total deliverance. He's the one that . . . God love and care so he sent his son Jesus all the way from glory, to come and hang on a tree for you and me, that we don't have to do it by our own selves. So God has already set the table for total deliverance, even preserving your family, you just didn't follow the instructions for keeping your family preserved. Seventh chapter of first Corinthians says:

> Now concerning the things whereof ye wrote unto me: it is good for a man not to touch a woman. Nevertheless to avoid fornication, let every man have his own wife, and let every woman have her own husband.

You see, I read that to say this. You left yourself open, according to your book, because when things wasn't going right between you and your wife, you allowed certain womens to creep into your life and [mumbled] with some of the church women that you knew . . . come in and spend nights with them and go to bed with 'em, and this wrong! And instead of you, when things were bad, falling on your knees and crying out to the Lord, you were looking for the bosom of another woman, which is a strange woman for you. Remember what the Lord said in the Book of Proverbs there . . . I'm gonna see what Proverbs . . . in what Scripture that is . . . in Proverbs . . . what the Lord is saying to you . . . why . . . why . . . that's the fifth chapter of Proverbs here . . . and uh . . . twentieth verse:

> And why wilt thou, my son, be ravished with a strange woman, and embrace the bosom of a stranger; for the ways of man are before the eyes of the Lord, and he pondereth all his goings.

See? You know, your wife might not have seen you, but God saw you. Alright? So you can't . . . you . . . you shouldn't have done

ϒ

things like that . . . you . . . ya stick . . . your OWN wife, your
OWN husband, the Lord saith . . . and there's Scriptures governing
what's what . . . who is your wife? And who is your husband? You
can't just grab up anybody and marry, see, because if I meet a woman
that has divorce her husband, and it wasn't for a case of fornication,
and it wasn't cause he said he didn't want her no more . . . if I
meet a woman that divorce her husband for any other reason other
than that, according to Scripture, she's not in liberty to marry another
man as long as he lives! So if I go marry her, and she has committed
this act of divorcing her husband, and it wasn't these reasons, I'm
in adultery! And so is she! I don't have my OWN wife, she doesn't
have her OWN husband. Matthew fifth chapter and the nineteenth
chapter talks about that, see, so, and . . . and divorcing in case of
fornication go first Corinthians, seventh chapter, around by the
fifteenth verse talk about divorcing. If the unbeliever depart, the
Lord says wife don't put away your unbelieving . . . don't divorce
your husband cause he's not saved. Don't put away your unbelieving
wife, don't divorce your wife cause she's not saved. But the Bible
says in that same Scripture . . . says: But if the unbelieving depart,
meaning if the one says they don't want the marriage no more,
and then find you fornicating, well, *they've become the unbeliever* because
the Bible says to remain together till death do you part. So, then,
that means that the one walking out is become an unbeliever . . . an
unbeliever means not believing what God is saying . . . the Bible
says that if the unbelieving depart, then the sister or brother is
not held bondage in such case. So the bond is cut for the one that
still wanted the marriage. But . . . the Bible says a sister or brother
is not held bondage. The unbeliever still have bondage. . . .

And just like that woman that Jesus met at the well, in the
fourth chapter of St. John, telling about her seventh . . . and asked
her about her husband, and she said, "I have none." Jesus tell her,
"Oh, you right, you had" . . . and he didn't say you, "just lived with
five men. . . . You have had five husbands, and the one, meaning
the husband you got now, is not yours." She was married to all
of them . . . she was married up with somebody else's husbands,
she didn't have her own husband. So let every man have his own
wife, and every woman her own husband. And that applies to me
and you . . . and we especially. You say . . . if . . . if you confess
and say you're preacher, it's especially . . . it is especially warranted
above for me and you to make sure we have our own husband

and own wife so we can be an example, and teach others. It's hard
to teach somebody one thing, when you doing another. I mean,
if your son and your family . . . and your daughters and your husband . . . there's a lot . . . and . . . or your wife . . . it's hard to tell
them that it's wrong to drink when you're coming home drunk!
See? You're gonna set confusion in your home. Well, if it's wrong
to drink, why'd Daddy come home drunk? See? Okay. So we want
to be the example and we want to teach the right thing. Uh . . .
I . . . uh . . . I had myself in bed with the wrong women in my
lifetime. I didn't know. Nobody taught me this Scripture and nobody
opened the Bible like this and taught it to me like this.

When I was growing up my mother thought that respect for
God was putting the Bible on the shelf and nobody touch it. "Children
keep your hands off it." She didn't know that respect in God was
givin' us Bibles and teaching us the Bible, because the Bible says:
Teach you children about me; when you're walking around with
'em, teaching about me when you sit in the rocker, when you sitting
down with 'em, teaching 'em when you get up in the morning,
teaching 'em when you putting them in bed at night. Let the signs
be all over your bedposts about me. So my mother didn't know
this and my daddy didn't know this . . . I mean they . . . like I said
. . . Momma would take the Bible and she gonna have that Bible
there, and to her respectin' it she put that Bible there "And don't
you touch it!" "You children leave this Bible alone" . . . and caught
you playing with the Bible and you got a whuppin'. Well, you see,
that was her way of respecting God, but that's not what God's
saying. The way of respecting God is teaching your children about
Him, and letting them walk there.

Alright. But so I didn't know. I . . . I . . . uh . . . committed all
these sins and all these wrongs . . . run around with women in my
lifetime. And when I accepted the ministry, that was one of the
reasons why I didn't wanta preach. I told God . . . I said God? . . .
(when the Lord gave me preaching) . . . I said Lord I do not wants
to preach. I said: Lord, you know that I love women. I love runnin'
around with women. I mean I will not be a hypocrite, Lord, so
I don't wanta preach. And God changed my mind about the thing
in a car accident. He'd called . . . now that was the third call He
had given me . . . that God sent. Don't let God call you three times
about the same thing . . . Good . . . God called you the first time.
Be wise and go on and answer Him and do what He tell you.

✗

But . . . get back to what I'm saying is . . . I didn't know, so when I accepted the ministry I had to get down and pray and pray and pray. I prayed and read my Bible day and night. I prayed so until I didn't . . . I didn't even . . . I couldn't eat and I couldn't sleep. I would wake up all times of night getting into that Bible. I went to sleep with that Bible on my chest, woke up with it on my chest. All times of night I'm praying and reading my Bible for the Lord to show me the right way.

And . . . and the thing about it is, when God showed me the way to go, I then started praying for the Lord to show me where my wife is. Ended up the woman I had wasn't her! And I had to get rid of her! And this woman (laughs) . . . and this woman here, was my childhood sweetheart! We went to school together. And that was the hardest thing for me to do! I just know . . . because that's the reason me and her together. For I just knew this was the woman. I'M SAYING THIS TO SAY THAT A LOT OF MAR-RIAGES TOGETHER HAVE TO DIVORCE FOR YOU TO GET RIGHT! Because you don't have your own wife and your own husband, see . . . but . . . but I prayed and prayed, and I told her about . . . about what the Scripture saith, and I prayed over seeing what I'm talking about. When you pray, God'll take care of the business if you will pray and let it . . . and I prayed and prayed to God, and God spoke to me about that thing and about the woman, and I wanted to know, and uh . . . and I left home one night and . . . uh . . . and what happen is . . . in praying, and this is the thing about it, the more I prayed for God to straighten out my life, the worse things was getting between me and this woman. But you see, God was answering my prayers. But I thought . . . I'm saying to myself, Lord, like the more I try to do right, the worse things getting with my life . . . and God was cleaning my life up (laughs) at the same time. I thought it was being MESSED up.

So I came home one day the woman had packed up and gone. I said, Lord, if this is . . . if this is my wife . . . if this is NOT my wife, then turn me around before I get there tonight . . . and the Lord gave me a sign to turn back before I got there. I talked to her. I'm talking about when you do this thing in . . . in the . . . the Lord and in His strength, and in His power . . . because you can't do it in your own power. What the Scripture saith, be strong in the power of His might, there is no defeat. So when you . . . when we do this in God's power, great things happen in truth . . . so the

✗

Lord showed me that she wasn't my own wife. And I talked to her about it, and told her what the Scriptures saith and when I TOLD her what the Scriptures saying about it, she did not fight me on it. She confessed to me, she say . . . I don't know the Scripture like you do, she said, but if what you tell me is true, then I'm not your wife. See, so God already worked it out. So I went to praying for the Lord to show me who she is. Good God Almighty! And God showed me, who she is. So . . . so the Lord is saying, let every man have his own wife. This is a serious matter! You . . . like . . . like one lady asked me, she said: "Well, Brother McKinney, won't God forgive me . . . if I got the wrong husband?" I said: "But how you going to get forgiveness for having the wrong husband if you're still together living with one another?" See, in other words . . . and having your affairs together . . . how can you get forgiveness for something that you're still doing?? You can't, because the first step in getting forgiveness of your sin is what? Repent. What repent means, turn away from your . . . turn to God and away from your sin. Well, if I don't turn to God and away from my sin, then how am I going to get forgiveness? You can't get forgiveness for something you're still . . . intend to stay in it . . . hmmmph . . . God almighty, that's a dangerous thing.

And when I thought about that thing, I thought, thinking how many people . . . in the world . . . don't know that they don't have their own husband, their own wife, because preachers will not preach ALL of the Gospel . . . preach that what sound good to the ear, preach that will brings money into the church because of . . . if I please my people sitting in the pews then they won't mind coming and the more people sitting there the more dollars there. I don't wanta say anything to hurt their feelings because I will lose . . . money. Good God Almighty! Let's get people saved . . . let's get the truth to people. So let every man have his own wife . . . let every woman have her own husband. I know . . . I mean . . . I . . . I can imagine . . . that you hadn't thought about all of that. In that one Scripture there before, because I tell'ya . . . man I prayed and read the Bible a long time before it all came to me. Let's look at Ephesians fifth chapter . . . when it came to me . . . for I tell 'ya it's in there, and God means what he says, and . . . and . . . like one man told me one day . . . he says, well? I mean . . . how do I know? . . . that ta . . . he say, then how do I know . . . uh . . . where my wife been? I mean is she been married before . . . now

X

. . . or she has somebody'll put me under . . . I mean I'm not . . . y"know . . . I mean . . . I suppose I ask her and she tell me a lie? Well, that's God, He's not gonna lie. The Bible wanta know, do I have my right wife? Well, uh . . . in my case I know . . . because I . . . uh . . . for God showed it to me before I married her. But if you find out the truth and already married to a woman, so why don't you pray and ask God? He's not gonna lie to you. He'll tell you. Hmmph! . . . God's been answering prayer before you and I was born. Abraham, Isaac and Jacob and Noah, and all these great *great Christians* back there. All these bu . . . our forefathers, they walked with God, he answered them, he didn't lie to them (laughs), he told 'em the truth. God will tell you the truth. If you think your husband or wife will lie to you, ask God. The problem is, we don't wanta get right enough to get the answer. Because it take righteousness to get answers from God, so what we wanta do? We're too lazy to do that. We're spiritually lazy. We're too spiritually lazy to get right with God, and yet, so . . . since . . . since I'm not gonna get right with God so he can give me an answer, I'll just go on as I am, with things as usual. Cause it's not worth it to take a chance on ending up in hell! I wanta know . . . do I have my own husband? . . . or my own wife? Alright. . . .

God say for man and wife become one, not the preacher and preaching become one, see? Men preaching don't become one, me and my wife become one, right? So, if . . . if they are certain things concerning my wife can stop me from going to preach, right. But preaching shouldn't stop me from doing the things that God says do for my wife. Because if I fail to do some things that God want me and have asked me to do for my wife, to go preach then, I'm not obeying the very word I'm preaching, because the Lord says to defraud her not . . . umm in first Corinthians seventh chapter, don't defraud ye one another. So don't keep things away from her that I'm suppose to do for her, as a matter of fact that Book of Proverbs that I was reading, about there where the Lord talk about . . . uh . . . be ravished by the breasts of your own wife . . . and all of that . . . where it talks about that also you know . . . that one thing the Lord say . . . you do these things for YOUR wife, your OWN wife. Why be ravished by the bosom of a stranger?? Now, alright, so let's . . . let's read on uh . . . uh . . . and get it over . . . I'm trying to get for the Lord his . . . has giving me to give you, Mark tenth chapter, first and twelfth verse, and this is . . . and

X

we're gonna talk about . . . marriage and divorce . . . is here again
. . . and we're gonna see clearly . . . what the Lord say about divorce.
Uh . . . we can't like I say before previously, you can't just
divorce . . . we can't just divorce a wife or a husband just because
we don't want 'em anymore and then just walk off and marry whoever
we wanta marry. Just doesn't work like that, in the Godly sight
of God . . . Mark the tenth chapter, first and twelfth verse, first
verse goes like this:

> And he arose from thence and cometh into the coasts of Judea
> by the farther side of Jordan; and the people resort unto him again:
> and, as he was wont, he taught them again. And the Pharisees
> came to him and asked him, is it lawful for a man to put away
> his wife? tempting him, and he answered and said unto them,
> What did Moses command you?

See? They always got people . . . they did it then, they're doing
it now, trying to tempt the man of God, the person that walking . . .
uh . . . upright in Christ Jesus and in God, and . . . he gets these
temptations.

> And they said, Moses suffered to write a bill of divorcement and
> to put her away. And Jesus answered and said unto the, for the
> hardness of your heart he wrote you this precept. But from the
> beginning of the creation God made them male and female. For
> this cause shall a man leave his father and mother, and cleave
> to his wife; and they twain shall be one flesh. So then they are
> no more twain, but one flesh. Wherefore . . . what therefore God
> hath joined together, let no man put asunder.

Now some people read that particular verse, the ninth verse, and
they say . . . oh . . . oh . . . they weren't meant to be cause if so,
I mean, they never would have parted, because God said what he
joined together LET no man put asunder. He didn't say you
COULDN'T do it . . . but the Scripture didn't say . . . God didn't
say; what I have joined together . . . and in no way you gonna be
able to pull it apart, he didn't say that. This Scripture is simply
giving instructions. What God put together don't bother with it
no more. Don't be trying to tear it apart. He didn't say you couldn't
do it, he asked us NOT to do it, because God said don't commit
adultery, too, but people still do it . . . see? . . . people still do it.

God said don't break up a marriage that he has put together, but people are breaking them up. Alright. So . . .

> And in the house his disciples asked him again of the same matter and he saith unto them, whose . . . whosoever shall put away his wife and marry another committeth adultery against her. And if a woman shall put away her husband, and be married to another, she committeth adultery.

Now this explains it from the Book of Mark more clearly than it does, that particular verse there, than it does in the Book of . . . uh . . . uh . . . . . Matthews, fifth chapter and nineteenth chapter. Because this spells it out plainer. If a man put away his wife, means divorce his wife and not for the cause of fornication, marry another, he committed adultery! and if woman divorce her husband and put him away, and marry another and not in the case of fornication, she commit adultery against her husband. And that's what I was talking about. So if . . . if . . . you walk up on somebody has done this, married before, put away their husband or wife weren't for this cause here, in the cause of first Corinthians, seventh chapter, that was given over there, those two, and you marry them, then you end up in adultery. So you don't have your own husband or your own wife . . . Christ come, or you die . . . find you like that, you're going to hell! Because you're living in adultery! You can't get forgiveness for adultery living in it . . . how can you? Amen. Amen. Alright.

Okay . . . let's go to uh . . . Ephesians sixth chapter, tenth through twentieth verses, . . . cause we need some power to hold us . . . to keep us from being tossed to and fro by the devil, and matter of fact, this what happened here uh . . . with you . . . what caused a lot of problems in your marriage . . . uh . . . here in Ephesians sixth chapter, ten:

> Finally my brethren, be strong in the Lord, and in the power of his might.

Not be strong in the power of the Assembly of God. Might . . . not in the power of your might . . . and not be strong in the power and the might of . . . RINGMASTER! But be strong in the power of God's might.

ʒ

> Put on the whole armor of God that ye may be able to stand against the wiles of the devil. For we wrestle not against flesh and blood, but against principalities, against powers, against the rulers of the darkness of this world, against spiritual weaknesses in high places. Wherefore take unto you the whole armor of God, that ye may be able to withstand in the evil day, and having done all to stand. Stand therefore having your loins girt about with truth, and having on the breastplate of righteousness; And your feet shod with the preparation of the gospel of peace; Above all, taking the shield of faith, wherewith ye shall be able to quench all the fiery darts of the wicked. And take the helmet of salvation, and the sword of the spirit, which is the word of God. Praying always with all prayer and supplication in the spirit, and watching thereunto with all perseverance and supplication for all saints.

Good God Almighty! So we need that . . . now I'm not gonna . . . now that's . . . that's easily understood, an . . . an . . . and you probably aware of it, but what you didn't do, you didn't put on the whole armor, and by not putting on the whole armor, it cost you a lot . . . cost you a lot. Cost you things that you don't seem to be able to get over. But I hope this will help you get over it. Well, Galatians first chapter and the tenth verse here . . . we're going to read that here, this is . . . this is the one that we're going to start . . . at the sixth verse here.

> I marvel that ye are so soon removed from him that called you unto the grace of Christ unto another gospel.

See? Which is not another Gospel!

> But there be some that trouble you, and would pervert the gospel of Christ. But though we or an angel from heaven preach any other gospel unto you than that which we have preached unto you, let him be accursed. As we said before, so say I now again, if any man preach any other gospel unto you than that ye have received let him be accursed. For do I now persuade men, or God? Or do I seek to please men? For if I yet please men, I should not be the servant of God.

See? For I gave you that Scripture for this purpose . . . uh . . . I don't know whether you was aware, but from reading your book you was seeking to please men more than pleasing God. Because

the moment you find out . . . you found out . . . that you found
out the Assembly of God organization was not all it was propped
up to be, and that it wasn't righteousness prevailing in the organization, you should have gotten out. But . . .but you . . . you stuck
with it because . . . like I said before . . . you all used one another.
The Assembly of God organization used you, and you used them.
You used the . . . got popularity in that vein too . . . to ride high
in ministry from day one, and . . . and instead of letting the Lord
build you up, growing in the Lord, you came in the . . . on the
minister scene . . . flying high already! Because of the Assembly of
God organization. They used you to draw crowds because of the
headlines . . . ringmaster become a preacher. A previous ringmaster
. . . uh . . . is now preaching at so and so . . . brings a crowd . . . got
a good ring to it. So you all used one another. So what you wanta
do is . . . you want to . . . come to God . . . on your knees . . .
confessing your sins . . . and start from scratch with God in sincerity and truth, and let GOD elevate you . . . let GOD exhalt
you . . . see, when men exhalt you, men can tear you down . . .
alright . . . but we have to ALLOW men to exhalt us for that to
happen. You know, they tried that with Paul. Paul said no. Paul
has screamed out to a man, rise up and walk. Because Paul perceived
that the man had faith enough to receive healing. And after that
the people in the town want to make Paul . . . wanted to exhalt
Paul and Barnabas, and Paul told them no, don't do that . . . in the
Book of Acts. Well, they wanted to do Peter the same way when
he went over to Cornelius . . . wanted to exhalt him . . . Paul . . .
uh . . . uh . . . an . . . PETER told Cornelius, stand up on your feet
for I'm just a man. You see, man cannot exhalt us unless we allow
him to: We ALLOW him to do it, then, we fall. You allowed the
Assembly of God organization to exhalt you, and they tumbled you
to the ground, see, they tumbled your ministry. They didn't tumble
your marriage. YOU tumbled your marriage . . . but they did tumble
your ministry. See, what you should have done, done like the
Scripture says . . . be ye separated, come out from among them,
touch not the unclean . . . isn't that what the Lord said? Be not
partaker of their sin so you will receive their plagues . . . eighteenth
chapter of Revelation, four and four. So you . . . you allowed it to
happen. You set yourself up for it. Don't mingle in it, what the
Scripture says I believe, in the Book of Psalms, what the Lord said
about it . . . not there . . . Proverbs it must be . . . How can a man

lay coals upon a chest . . . what? . . . when it's not burning, how can a man walk on coals, what? . . . and his feet not burn. See . . . you . . . you messing around in that mess that they have going, and it'll get you! What it's in the sixth chapter of Proverbs there, twenty-seventh verse . . . Can a man take fire in his bosom and his clothes not be burned? Could you stay there mingling among the Assemblies of God organization and knowing they wasn't right? And then you gotta end up destroyed? Can one go upon hot coals and his feet not be burned? No you can't do it! You can't do it. You stay in it, it gets ya. You . . . you stay among pigs, and you'll smell like pigs. You walk in the mud, you get muddy. There's no way you can walk in the mud and not get muddy. You walk in the rain, you get wet. That's why when the Lord said to come out from among them . . . touch not the unclean . . . come out from among them. Don't blame God. Don't blame the Assembly of God denomination . . . uh . . . just confess your sin before God, and be cleansed from your sins. The Lord has promised to wash you, and you shall be whiter than snow.

We thank God for the privilege of bringing you this message, and we just wanta pray right here and bring an end to this particular taping:

> Our Father in the name of Jesus . . . we stand before your throne in behalf of Mr. Austin Miles, God Almighty we pray . . .that the anointing of you will be upon him . . . for strong deliverance . . . powerful deliverance, real deliverance . . . FROM THE SPIRIT OF CIRCUS RINGMASTER . . . that you have greater things for him than THAT. Oh, God Almighty, we thank you for blotting out our transgressions. Thank you for cleansing us from all our iniquity. And thank you for healing us . . . from all sickness and disease and from all sin and all evil. Thank you for delivering us from wickedness. Thank you for the forgiveness of sins. Father, in the name of Jesus, we give you the praise and the glory and the honor right now for your word. Hallelujah! And for the deliverance of your word . . . in power . . . in the name of Jesus. Amen . . . and amen."

I listened to this taped sermon in my car while returning home from Los Angeles after doing radio interviews with Tom Leykis of KFI and John Steward of KKLA. The next morning in Northern California I was scheduled to check into the hospital for my cancer operation. However, before doing that, I dropped a quick note to "Brother" McKinney to suggest to him that the god who "told him to preach that sermon to me" was undoubtedly the same god who told Pat Robertson that he was going to be president and Oral Roberts that if his flock didn't cough up 8.5 million dollars, he would be yanked out of this world.

XII

Christian Influence
on Society

X   Train up a child in the way he should go; and when he is old,
    he will not depart from it.

Proverbs 22:6

The churches would have us believe that their existence improves
society around them. If this is so, I haven't seen the slightest bit
of evidence to support it. The pressure that fundamentalist churches
have placed on our school system has succeeded in driving American
educational standards to an alarmingly low level. The militant religious right has tampered with textbooks, retarded scientific study
(and in some cases tried to eliminate it altogether), and discouraged
students from reading many of the classics. Moreover, the insistence
of the fundamentalist churches on having creationism taught in science classes takes time and space away from the teaching of real
science.

By the end of this century, it is estimated that church meddling
and outright interference in our educational system will cost America
400,000 Ph.D.-level scientists and 1.6 million bachelor's degrees in
the sciences. According to syndicated columnist Thomas D. Elias,
the resultant scientific shortfall is already upon us, being filled in
large part by scientists imported from countries like England, China,
Yugoslavia, and India. Key engineering, technical, and policy-making
jobs—even in defense industries—are being filled by immigrants,
some of whom are not yet citizens.

The fundamentalist churches are dragging our children, the future generations, down to a level acceptable to *them*. Meanwhile, non-Christian-dominated countries are bypassing America in the development of scientific and commercial resources.

Most evangelicals are opposed to education, period. The more education one possesses, the less likely can one be manipulated and controlled. One of the scriptural authorities the Christians cite to discourage education is Romans 1:22; "Professing themselves to be wise, they became fools."

Here is what the late Rev. William Branham said about education in his publication, *The Lord Hath Spoken:* "Education, and the educational system, science, and civilization is of the devil. It's the devil's civilization. The Bible said so." As shown in the "Blaspheous" section of this book, the devoted followers of Rev. Branham embody his theory.

In the former totalitarian government of Romania, Nicolae Ceausescu forbade abortions for any woman with fewer than five children. The result, according to Dr. Patti Subtirelu, director of the gynecological and obstetric clinic of the Colea Hospital in Bucharest: "The dignity of the woman really vanished. The women are looked on as breeding animals." The most pointed comment came from Florica Iosifescu, a Romanian who had an abortion after the execution of Ceausescu: "Ceausescu made this anti-abortion rule on purpose to make us like animals. He wanted more children only as labor to continue to work for him."

The same could be said about the church in the rest of the world. Despite overpopulation problems, which threaten the very existence of the human race, the church says, ready or not, keep having babies, under any and all conditions.

The most outrageous case of Christian meddling concerning the abortion issue took place on December 13, 1988. Martin Klein of New York and his pregnant wife Nancy were involved in a horrible car accident that left Mrs. Klein in a coma. An abortion was planned for the comatose wife, whose pregnancy placed her possible recovery in jeopardy. Christian abortion foes forced their way into these people's lives, which were already wracked with tragedy. They filed a lawsuit to prevent the abortion from taking place. Mr. Klein had to fight these nitwits all the way to the Supreme Court before finally being allowed to have the abortion performed.

As a result of overpopulation, we have run out of space to dump our garbage; we have polluted the air, the rivers, and now even the ocean. Our desperate efforts to protect the environment have been met with opposition from the religious right. James Watt, a born-again evangelical who sat on the board of directors of the scandalous PTL Club ministry while serving as our Secretary of Interior, said *this* about the environment: "God gave us these things to use. After the last tree is felled, Christ will come back." This "end of the world is near, so just use everything" mentality is echoed by Jerry Falwell and Pat Robertson, among others, on the forefront of the Christian right.

The very history of the church is written with blood and destruction. One of the darkest times in the history of civilization was the period of the Inquisition, when Catholic priests used torture to punish and force suspected heretics to submit to church doctrine. During that time, a bishop wrote to the pope: "We're so pious in our village that even if we *suspect* someone is a heretic, we burn them at the stake!"

There is no way that any organization that promotes hatred, division, and disruption can be considered beneficial to society. Why do we sanction, with tax-free privileges, *any* organization that is taught to hate? Yes, Christians *are* taught to hate, every time they gather in their tax-free churches. I know because I was once one of them. First they are taught to hate the devil. . . Lucifer . . . Satan. Which brings up a stinging question. If Christians serve a forgiving God, then how is it that God, and His followers, show no inclination to forgive the devil? Satan, according to the Bible, was originally an angel of God, one of His elect, but along the way he rebelled. Many of us who were part of the system have rebelled but are told we can be forgiven. So why would God not forgive the devil? This alone contradicts the validity of Christian theology. Why have we missed this?

As Christians are taught to hate Satan, they can then transfer this divinely sanctioned hatred to any and all who will not become one of their number. "If they are not with us, they are against us." Everything and everyone in disagreement with the born-agains and their churches is of the devil. Even a painful, revealed truth is in the eyes of the faithful the work of the devil to discourage them.

So the devil-hatred becomes transferred to those who disagree with the Christian belief system or who disrupt their ceremonies. This even includes their own innocent babies! During a Richard Roberts telecast on January 16, 1990, a guest pastor declared that during a Christian service witches pray that babies will cry to disrupt the message. This, he said, had been revealed to him in a telephone conversation with a leading satanist who would not give his name. "And," saith the pastor, "I can confirm this." It takes little imagination, considering the brainwashed condition of the born-again Christian, to see how such teaching could lead to child abuse.

Today, when someone says to me, "I'm a born again Christian," I say, "Thanks for the warning." They mean to impress me, but such a statement has an opposite effect on me. What he is basically saying to me is: "I no longer take any personal responsibility for my actions. Now I can effectively blame God or the devil for any of my character flaws. I can cloak my natural instincts in the mantle of Christianity, and that will make it all right. Praise the Lord!"

I think of born-again Christians like Jim Jones, Jim Bakker, Jimmy Swaggart, and Oral Roberts. I think of these egocentric misfits who use their "born-again" status to rise on the ladder of power over the "spiritually ignorant." Even the destruction of a family proves that they are able to affect *something* in life, making them feel powerful and important.

The public is continually fed propaganda regarding the wonderful way in which Christianity changes lives. There is not one case on the record to prove that Christianity changes lives. There is not one case on record to prove that Christianity has actually caused a personality change. There are of course some very good Christians along with some very bad ones. Usually, both have extreme personalities. There is rarely one in between. *Christianity does not change lives. It simply magnifies what the person already is.* This is why Christian personalities are abnormal and often border on the fanatic.

The church of Jesus Christ has no defense against this book. It is filled with the voices of the people relating a continuing saga of the destruction of lives at the hands of the church; the systematic break-up of families; rape; child molestation; suicide; nervous breakdowns; and death due to church-encouraged neglect of medical treatment. The tragedy is that the victims of the church would never have been victims had they not submitted themselves to the voluntary slavery that *is* the church of Jesus Christ. Many of the victims would be alive today and productive citizens had they avoided church influence. This institution known as the church, which throughout history has caused only terror and mischief, must be reformed, with constant supervision, or it must be brought to an end for the sake of society.

The concept of religious freedom has exceeded its limits, to the detriment of society. I am all for the church. That's where the Christians belong. Keep them there. At least we will know where they are. Just don't turn them loose on society, and especially on our children in school.

The most remarkable truth to the churches' teachings is the preacher's concept of Satan, "coming as an angel of light, but causing derision, confusion, and division." That definition perfectly fits the church itself. Perhaps the so-called Christian church and Satan are the same. Evidence would certainly make a strong case for that possibility.

I am not against God. I am against what man has made God out to be: an instrument to feed his own natural aggression and instinct to conquer his fellow man and put him into subjection; a tool for greed, self-enrichment, power, and control; a means to further his desire for grandeur and adulation; the ultimate power base in which sin, evil deeds, war, and even torture can be explained away by the Bible itself.

I am against what man has done to the Bible, interpreting and rewriting its "message" over the centuries so that the power would be in man's hands instead of God's. It has become the greatest fraud the world has ever known, and has had profoundly evil consequences in the history of peoples and nations.

One does not find God through man-made church rituals. God is only found in the individual heart. I would like to ask God one day if He ever felt that it was a mistake to give man free will. I believe He would say to me, with sadness in His voice, "Possibly so. Possibly no. I gave man the power to heal . . . but he never used it."

Index